New Light
on
The New Testament

An account of some interesting discoveries which bear important testimony as to the time when the gospels and other books of the New Testament were written.

By
PARKE P. FLOURNOY, D D
Author of " The Search-Light of Hippolytus "

INTRODUCTION BY
PROF BENJ B WARFIELD, D D , LL D

WIPF & STOCK · Eugene, Oregon

Wipf and Stock Publishers
199 W 8th Ave, Suite 3
Eugene, OR 97401

New Light on the New Testament
An Account of Some Interesting Discoveries
Which Bear Important Testimony as to the Time
When the Gospels and Other Books of the New
Testament Were Written
By Flournoy, Parke P. and Warfield, Benjamin B.
Softcover ISBN-13: 978-1-6667-0448-8
Hardcover ISBN-13: 978-1-6667-0449-5
eBook ISBN-13: 978-1-6667-0450-1
Publication date 3/5/2021
Previously published by The Westminster Press, 1903

This edition is a scanned facsimile of
the original edition published in 1903.

Contents

	PAGE
PREFATORY NOTE	v
INTRODUCTION (Prof. Benj. B Warfield, D. D., LL D.)	vii

CHAPTER I
FALSE LIGHTS THAT LEAD ASTRAY 1

CHAPTER II.
NEW LIGHT ON A MARTYR'S TESTIMONY . . . 18

CHAPTER III.
THE GREAT LIGHT FROM THE VATICAN 47

CHAPTER IV.
THE FULLER LIGHT FROM MOUNT SINAI . . . 84

CHAPTER V.
TWIN LIGHTS FROM ATHENS 111

CHAPTER VI.
LIGHT FROM THE LAND OF THE PHARAOHS . . 136

CHAPTER VII.
MANY LIGHTS FROM MANY LANDS OR LIGHT ON THE SETTING 157

APPENDIX 179

Prefatory Note

I WAS encouraged to publish, in the present form, the following accounts of discoveries by the opinion kindly expressed by Dr. Warfield of Princeton Theological Seminary and Dr. Hersman of Union Theological Seminary, Richmond, Va., of an article published in the *Presbyterian Quarterly* on the three earliest apologists. They both urged me to put into book form this and other articles on discoveries which of late years have made clearer than ever the proof of the traditional dates of the gospels and other books of the New Testament.

To every reader I would say that I have not only found much pleasure in the studies of which this little book is the fruit, but have been brought to feel more fully than ever before the *certainty* of those things wherein we have been instructed about Christ our Lord.

My wish for every reader is that, more firmly and joyously than ever before, he may believe that Jesus is the Christ, the Son of God; and, believing, may have life through his name.

PARKE P. FLOURNOY.

The Manse, Bethesda, Md., Jan. 21, 1903.

Introduction

BY PROF. BENJ. B. WARFIELD, D. D., LL. D.
PRINCETON THEOLOGICAL SEMINARY

THE age in which our lot is cast, is an age of very eager research. It has had its reward in a long list of discoveries in every department of knowledge. Its scientific achievements can scarcely be said to have come " without observation." Its historical and literary discoveries have naturally lain a little more out of the range of the public view. Even some of these, it is true, have been too epoch-making to remain hidden. When Dr. Schliemann's pick dug out Troy from the superincumbent ages, and at Mycenæ gave us back a whole forgotten culture, a thrill went through the whole civilized world : the several stages in the recovery of the records of the great Mesopotamian empires have been watched with even intenser interest by even greater multitudes Nor can any undue modesty be attributed to the investigators in these recondite fields, leading them to underestimate the importance of their "finds" or to refrain from calling public attention to them. Exploitation of the results of research has often been as eager as the research itself. A certain kind of knowledge of these results has accordingly become very widespread. Not merely has "Babel and Bible" become a familiar alliteration, but such outlandish names as Oxyrhynchus and Akhmim lisp on the lips of babes.

Sometimes this exploitation of results is in inverse ratio to the value of the discovery proclaimed. Incredible efforts are made to give immense significance to the veriest trifles, and a deafening clamor is raised over every scrap of papyrus dug out of the dust-heaps of Egypt. A fragment scarcely two inches square containing a sentence from some old homily, long, and doubtless very happily, forgotten, is heralded over the world as a portion of a "precanonical gospel," with startling intimations of the ruin its discovery is to work in the authority of our presently accepted gospels. A but little larger fragment containing a series of exceedingly apocryphal "sayings of Jesus," is sensationally published with the grossly misleading title of "Logia of

Jesus" affixed to it, and the suggestion made that we have recovered in it something at least very similar to the "Logia" which Papias attributed to Matthew,—though this old writer certainly meant just our Gospel of Matthew by this designation, despite the efforts of a certain type of criticism to make him mean something else.

The *cognoscenti* may smile at such obviously despairing attempts at the creation out of nothing of support for insupportable theories. But what is the uninformed public to think of it all? Ignorant of the real state of affairs, and startled out of its indifference by the exploitation of such discoveries as these, a certain uneasiness is growing up among us, and Babylon bids fair to become again a name of dread and Egypt a land from whose sands may be expected to spring up any day a monster to devour us. There is great need that some one should tell the people plainly and with a sufficient body of illustration what have been the real results of the investigations of the last quarter of a century, and what is the real bearing they have on the documents of our faith. It is this service that Dr. Flournoy is rendering, first in his excellent *Searchlight of St. Hippolytus* published a few years ago, and now again in the present volume.

Paradoxical as it may sound, it is easy both to overestimate and to underestimate the importance of such discoveries as Dr. Flournoy recounts to us in this interesting narrative.

It is easy to overestimate their importance. It is a very unwholesome state of mind which is always groping for "confirmations" of the genuineness, trustworthiness or authority of our sacred writings. And it is as unjustified as it is unwholesome. We have not accepted these writings as authentic documents of the apostolic age and the infallible word of God, on flimsy grounds. We need no new evidence to establish them in our confidence. The mass and cogency of the evidence already in hand is so great, indeed, that it simulates infinity and hardly admits of substantial increase. Carrying coals to Newcastle is proverbially unimportant labor. He who is seeking for new items of evidence, may certainly find them, and there is no reason why he should not rejoice in them: but it is all very much a work of supererogation.

Even more may perhaps be fitly said. Search we never so diligently, we need not expect to find anything in itself of palmary importance. The Christian Church in her course through the ages has not dropped out of her knowledge the things that made most for her stability and peace. Most of the documents that have been lost have been lost because they were comparatively not much worth keeping. Accordingly most of the documents that can be found, we could do very well without finding. What has been specially worth preserving has been, as a rule, specially carefully preserved. The enthusiasm of discovery sometimes leads scholars to talk of "revolutions" that are to be wrought by the documents they have brought to light. It is a perhaps not unnatural illusion. When the enthusiasm of discovery cools and normal judgment reasserts itself, it will be found that the balance hangs at much its old angle. The lineaments of the primitive church, drawn on the credit of the major documents that have been kept in the continuous possession of men, will not be much altered on the faith of the minor documents that have for a time passed out of notice.

We need only to ask ourselves what important gains for the chief concerns of the faith have accrued to us from the most interesting of recent discoveries, to perceive clearly how subordinate a rôle they must play. What do we learn from the Akhmim fragment concerning the composition or history of our gospels? Practically nothing. What new information as to the original form or authority of our gospels does the Lewis palimpsest bring us? None whatever. What new fact of importance do we gain for the early history of the gospels in the church from the recovery of Tatian's *Diatessaron?* Not one. We knew before its recovery that the *Diatessaron* was just a harmony of our four gospels; and on its recovery it is naturally seen to be just a harmony of our four gospels. The absurdity of denying it to be just a harmony of our four gospels was practically as great before as it is after its recovery: and its recovery has not rendered it impossible for absurd men to continue to perpetrate absurdity. The author of *Supernatural Religion*, in his new edition published last year, still denies the *Diatessaron* to be a simple harmony of our gospels: he says the discovered harmony is not Tatian's.

It is really impossible to correct foregone conclusions by multiplication of evidence. What overwhelming evidence will not accomplish, still more overwhelming evidence will no more accomplish. A man submerged under a hundred fathoms of water will be no more drowned if you make it five hundred. Even if somebody should draw out of some hiding-place, to-morrow, a complete copy of Papias' *Expositions of the Oracles of the Lord*, which is perhaps the most interesting of very early Christian documents yet awaiting recovery, there is no reason to believe that we should reap substantial evidential gains from its recovery. Anybody who wishes to know, can know now what the book was. And anybody who wishes absurdly to deny that it was what it was, could still deny it, with the book in his hand, as reasonably as he can now. Those whom sufficient evidence will not convince, will not be convinced by a resurrection from the dead. It is vain to hope that the task of Christian Apologetics will be substantially lightened by discoveries of this kind. The difficulty of the task of Christian Apologetics does not arise from insufficiency in the evidence it is prepared to offer. It lies in a very different quarter.

But, on the other hand, as we have said, it is very easy to underestimate the importance of discoveries of this kind. The term "importance" is a relative term, and there needs to be asked on each occasion of its employment, "Of importance for what?" Is the difference of a thousandth part of an inch between two measurements of importance? That depends on what we are measuring and for what end. Out in the fields, where we are measuring the stone-fence which is to be paid for at so much a rod, it is of no importance whatever. It is of no importance to the drygoods clerk who is measuring off a dozen yards of muslin for a customer's dress. In the observatory where the astronomer is measuring the parallax of a fixed star, it is, however, of the utmost importance. An error of this dimension in this measurement is nothing less than immense. Micrometers are of no use whatever in the ordinary concerns of life, and the intrusion of them into that sphere would not only be an impertinence but an intolerable nuisance. They nevertheless in their own sphere of usefulness possess an importance that is literally inestimable.

Somewhat similarly, discoveries in the domain of early Christian literature which have no importance for the life and faith of the Christian Church may yet each have a very large importance in the appropriate sphere of investigation to which it belongs. The discovery of the Lewis palimpsest, for example, cannot be said to possess any significance for the Christian life. But it has high importance for the history of the Syriac Bible. Some very interesting outstanding questions in that sphere of investigation, it goes far toward settling; and it raises some new problems of its own which the student finds exceedingly interesting and full of meaning. It even has some importance, through its significance for the history of the Syriac Bible, for the history of the text of the New Testament; and thus plays its part in the laborious task of the ascertainment of the exact text of the New Testament. It is easy to exaggerate the part it plays in this great work, and some very strange things have been said about it in this relation—which, however, can be easily pardoned the enthusiasm of discovery. Similarly Tischendorf, when he found the great Codex Sinaiticus, in the first flush of exhilaration lost temporarily the balance of his judgment and was inclined to treat it as the decisive witness to the New Testament text. He even published an edition of his New Testament in which the readings of the new codex were given preponderating authority. A very few years sufficed to correct his error and to readjust the relative values of the witnessing documents more equitably.

What we need most particularly to bear in mind, however, is that in all matters of this kind we are in a region in which measurements are taken with a micrometer. When we speak of things important and unimportant for textual criticism, for instance, we are talking in terms of a scale of measurements which has no application and no meaning in the domain of common life. There is no extant text of the New Testament that is not abundantly pure for our ordinary use, as we strive to build ourselves up in our most holy faith, and to furnish ourselves completely unto every good work. But the textual critic operates with other standards, and to him it is a matter of importance which of two prepositions meaning "from" is used in a given passage or how an aorist verb is spelled,—whether after the so-called "Alexandrian" fashion with an "a," or after the so-called "Classical" style, with an "o." It is of high importance for him, investigating such things, to ascertain what was the type of Greek text that underlies the earliest Syriac translation; and as the Lewis palimpsest helps him notably in this investigation, it appeals to him as a highly important discovery.

Similarly measured by the micrometer of detailed investigation, each new discovery in the domain of early Christendom has its own high value. Do we wish, for example, to work out the history of the subterraneous literature of primitive Christianity,—the literature that represented in that time the publications in our day of Dowieism and Christian Science and Mormonism? To the student in this department of research, the Akhmim fragment, the Oxyrhynchus papyrus, and the like, commend themselves as most important discoveries. Do we wish to work out the detailed history of the conflict of early Christianity with the civil authorities, in its effort to make standing room for itself in the world? Then the discovery of Aristides' *Apology* will appeal to us as of quite exceptional importance. Are our studies given to tracing out the history of the comparative study of the gospels? Then the recovery of the text of Tatian's harmony, even in a translated and somewhat revised shape, will be hailed by us as of the utmost value.

Of course no department of Christian study, any more than any Christian himself, stands off to itself in isolation from all other departments. Each works in with all the others in the complex activity of the Christian scholarship of the day, as it strives to perfect its multiform task of thoroughly exploring the history of the founding and growth of our religion in the world. What is important for any one of them, therefore, is through it important for the total which their sum makes up; and, through it, for the whole intellectual life of organized Christianity. Accordingly, the intelligent Christian sympathetically feels the importance of each and everything that any Christian worker in any sphere of investigation finds important for his work. Only we must guard ourselves from transmuting its relative importance into an absolute importance, under a different scale of measurements, and thus coming to fancy that in some way Christianity itself hangs on it.

This is not to say that these discoveries have no apologetical value. It is to say that it is important that their apologetical value should be truly estimated. For this, it is necessary to remind ourselves of the real apologetical situation. This, as has been already hinted, is the precise opposite of apologetical dearth. The constant conflict that necessarily reigns in a department the very function of which is conflict, is the result of the continual repetition of the following process. Some thinker, unwilling to believe in the supernatural character and origin of Christianity, as evinced in the evidence marshaled by the apologist, asks himself how he can reconstruct the factors that entered into the origin and development of Christianity so as to present it as a natural product. He carefully constructs for himself a hypothetical history of its origin and growth with the omission of all supernatural factors, seeking to rearrange the facts of history so as to permit this. In doing so he comes into repeated conflict with the facts as witnessed by the testimony in hand. He is thus led artificially to manipulate this testimony, in order to escape the supernaturalistic implication. Thus he builds up an elaborate structure, on which not only the most wide and accurate learning but shining talents and often genius itself have been expended. In the process, he has, for example, plausibly explained away all the evidence that Tatian's *Diatessaron* was a harmony of our four gospels: suggesting a doubt here, intruding a brilliant conjecture there, presenting a new interpretation there, and so manipulating the whole that his readers are almost ready to disbelieve the testimony of their own eyes and accept instead this fairy-tale as truth. Then Tatian's *Diatessaron* suddenly turns up and clears the atmosphere. Nothing really new has been discovered. It was perfectly well known before just what the *Diatessaron* was. But men's confused minds have been clarified; all the plausible reasoning by which they were in danger of being deceived is swept away; and things are allowed to fall back into their old and proper places.

Now just this process has been going on over and over again, until it has become a classical remark that every new discovery drives a new nail into the coffin of critical unbelief. The metaphor is a peculiarly happy one. It implies that critical unbelief is already, rightly viewed, dead and safely encoffined: and it takes note that the progress of research has only been steadily driving superfluous nail after superfluous nail into the lid. That lid must be pretty nearly all nails by now.

It is, however, not nearly so widely known as it ought to be that this is the precise state of the case. And it is just here that these excellent books of Dr. Flournoy's have their function. They come forward to tell the busy Christian who has had little time to inform himself at first-hand of the real condition of affairs, precisely how things really are. It is a very important service that Dr. Flournoy is thus rendering the Church: and he is doing it admirably. We owe him our thanks for it; and we accord them to him most heartily.

Princeton, February 1, 1903.

I.

FALSE LIGHTS THAT LEAD ASTRAY

I. THE OLD FRENCH TEACHER AND HIS STARTLING ASSERTION

IN Richmond, Virginia, for many years before the Civil War, there stood, or more properly, sat, a rather strange-looking, one-storied, wooden building, with a little sign over the door, on which were inscribed, if I remember aright, the words, "Select Classical School." In it was to be found during the day, except at mealtimes, and even before day and late into the night, an indefatigable worker—a rather short, muscular man of peculiar appearance and manners. He was one of that army of teachers from New England that invaded the South long before the cry "On to Richmond" was raised by an army of a very different kind. The South owes a great debt of gratitude to these teachers, who side by side with those educated in southern colleges and universities, did the great work of dispensing the priceless benefits of preparatory education in advance of the organization of a public-school system.

This one was a good, earnest, Christian man. He had his faults, no doubt (and who of us has not some of his own?), but, except for some infirmities—or the opposite—of temper, David Turner lived for thirty or forty years in Richmond an unusually blameless and eminently useful life. The scholars who went from his school to the University of Virginia, there to attain to the degree of A. M., and thence to Germany, whence they returned with Ph. D. added to their names, were his pride; and he never failed to keep the eyes of those under his ferule on the noble heights which these heroes had gained. There must be many elderly men, reared in Richmond during those years, who remember with gratitude the earnest exhortations and careful training of this faithful teacher.

In the modern language department of this school there presided, during certain hours of the day, an old Frenchman, Monsieur Michard, no less remarkable in appearance and other characteristics than his chief. He was a wizened, wrinkled mite of a man, looking, as he went out of the door on a March day, wrapping his old surtout about his emaciated form,

False Lights That Lead Astray 3

as if the wind would actually take him up and blow him away like the last leaf of autumn. He had been a lawyer, long ago, in Lyons, he told us; and for political reasons, had found it convenient, if not absolutely necessary, to leave his native land. Conversation was by no means forbidden in the modern language room when the lesson was through with before the hour was out, and M. Michard did not disdain to regale the inquiring minds of his pupils with other things besides the French and Spanish languages which he had to teach them. He was a Roman Catholic, and as often happens in the case of educated men in that communion, there was in him the strange combination of a certain kind of devoutness with skepticism.

One day he astonished at least one of his pupils by saying, in effect, that the New Testament could hardly be a divine revelation, because, as he asserted, besides the writings of which it was composed, there were perhaps a hundred others about as good as those which had been collected and made into the New Testament.

Providentially, an antidote was at hand. Richmond was favored with the ministry of the gifted and devoted Dr. Thomas Verner Moore at that time, and the troubled pupil found, under his ministry, a great deliverance from a terrible fate through the gospel contained in that very New Testament on which the old teacher had cast these aspersions. He felt that it must be of God, as it brought that help in dire extremity which nothing else could furnish, and which nothing else had the slightest tendency to furnish. The conviction he had was like that of the starving man when food has been brought to save his life and he has felt its reviving and sustaining power from the first morsel he has taken. Finding, by his own experience, this gospel to be "the power of God unto salvation," he could not help believing that the book containing it was of God.

This incident, however, has caused that pupil of the old Frenchman to take a deep interest in several recent discoveries which have shown very clearly the falsity of the old man's assertion and of the implication contained in it.

His feeling, on coming to know, in later life, of the evidence from early Christian literature that this assertion had only a specious basis in the existence from an earlier or later time of a large number of "pious frauds" going under the general name of New Testament Apocrypha, which were never universally received

False Lights That Lead Astray 5

by the Church as inspired, was one of relief. When, in more recent years, discoveries were made which completely vindicated the genuineness of the New Testament writings, and especially the four gospels, his feeling was like what that of a son might be whose father had died under false accusations—which he could not disprove, though absolutely sure from his knowledge of his father's character that they were false—when, among that father's papers he had found the full proof of his innocence and could publish it to the world.

II. HAECKEL AND THE GOSPELS

The assertion of M. Michard about the selection of the New Testament books from a large number of similar writings was probably based on a story which has long been a favorite article of the stock-in-trade of infidels who make pretensions to learning, and which has been repeated in various forms in a large number of publications. A version of it may be found in the *American Review of Reviews* of only a few years ago, in an article entitled "How the Bible Came Down to Us," and one meets with it in the most unexpected places. Opening the recent work of Professor Haeckel, of Berlin, the corypheus of the host of atheistic evolutionists who have made so much unmelodious noise in the world—and about the world—for the last half century and more, I was surprised to find the great scientist repeating the absurd story in the pages of his *Riddle of the Universe.* This is his version of it (p. 311): "As to the four canonical gospels, we now know that they were selected from a host of contradictory, and forged manuscripts of the first three centuries by the three hundred and eighteen bishops who assembled at the council of Nicæa in 327 [sic]. The entire list of gospels numbered forty, and the canonical list contains four. As the contending and mutually abusive bishops could not agree about the choice, they determined to leave the selection to a miracle. They put all the books (according to the Synodicon of Pappus), together underneath the altar, and prayed that the uncanonical books, of human origin, might remain there, and the genuine inspired books might be miraculously placed on the table of the Lord. And that, says tradition, occurred! The three synoptic Gospels, Matthew, Mark and Luke—all written after them, and not by them, at the beginning of the second century, and the very different Fourth Gospel (ostensibly "after" John, written about the middle of the

False Lights That Lead Astray 7

second century) leaped upon the table and were thenceforth recognized as the inspired (with their thousand mutual contradictions) foundations of Christian doctrine." He then goes on with sarcastic and violent raillery at Christians who could be so senseless as to believe in the uncouth miracle.

Now if before printing this nonsense, Haeckel had been prudent enough to go to some one well-informed about such matters—to Prof. Adolf Harnack, in the theological department of the great Berlin University, for instance—and tell him of it, he would probably have said, had politeness allowed, something like this:—

"My venerable friend, it would be wisest for us to confine ourselves to our own departments of investigation, as it is best for the shoemaker to stick to his last. Had I gone to you and told you that through scientific discoveries in this universe, of which you seem to have solved the riddle, 'we now know' that the moon is made of green cheese, and must, therefore, of course, be inhabited, I should not have made myself more ridiculous than you would make yourself by publishing this. For, in the first place, there is no evidence that the Council of Nice did anything at all in the way of settling the Canon of Scripture. The story you repeat is a baseless mediæval legend.[1] In the second place, abundant quotations in Irenæus from the four gospels as well as distinct statements on the subject, show that the four gospels were as fully accepted in the year two hundred, as the only inspired accounts of our Saviour's life on earth, as they are now; while Justin Martyr shows by his quotations from these "*Memoirs of the Apostles*" as he calls them, that the case was just the same more than fifty years earlier. Besides this, we now have, by recent discovery, the four gospels wrought into a continuous account in Tatian's *Diatessaron* (*i e.*, through four), the very name of which shows that there were but four gospels recog-

---

[1] "There is not the slightest evidence that the Council of Nice had anything whatever to do with settling the Canon of the New Testament It was not called for any such purpose, nothing relating to the subject appears in the canons or acts of the council, no writer of the fourth, or fifth, or sixth, or seventh, or eighth century has even hinted that the matter came before the council in any way"—*Dr. Ezra Abbot.*

The story was published by John Pappus, of Strasburg, at the beginning of the 17th century, from an anonymous manuscript which mentioned events occurring in A D. 869, "500 years after the members of the Nicene council were dead and buried," as one has well said, and is a companion piece of many such monkish stories of uncouth miracles It may be found republished in Fabricius' *Bibliotheca Græca*, Vol. XI, p 198.

nized, fifty years after the death of the Apostle John; and by necessary implication, there had been no others thus recognized by the Christian Church. Besides all this, we now have the four gospels in Syriac, complete, with the exception of a few pages lost out of the manuscript, earlier still than this *Diatessaron*, as is thought, because the *Diatessaron* contains many of its peculiar readings. It would be best, dear friend, for you to go on solving universe riddles and leave these matters to persons who have some information about early Christianity."

Professor Haeckel's mistake is due to his ignorance of the fact that the positions of the famous Tübingen School,[1] so boldly maintained by unbelieving scholars till twenty-five years ago, have been made absolutely untenable by recent discoveries; and now, no one who is informed on the subject can believe either in the late origin of any of the four gospels, or in the universal acceptance, at any time, of any of the many heretical gospels so-called. The *Gospel of Peter*[2], so-called, fragments of which

---

[1] Haeckel, while modifying Baur's dates, emphasizes his conclusions as to the spuriousness of the gospels
[2] See Ante-Nicene Fathers, IX Vol, pp. 3–31 Harnack assigns it to the first quarter of the second century Other scholars place it later

were discovered a few years ago at Akhmim, in Egypt, seems to be a Docetic document, dependent on, and in its main structure, patterned after, our gospels. The Apocryphal *Gospel according to the Hebrews*, which, possibly, originated still earlier than that of Peter,[1] was used by the heretical sects of the Ebionites, and Nazarenes and shows plainly, in the twenty-three quotations from it which are extant, dependence on all four of our gospels.[2] So it comes about that these, the two oldest, apparently, of all the false gospels that are known, when closely examined, become witnesses for the four gospels instead of competitors with them.[3]

---

[1] Dr Theodor Zahn says, (Einleitung, I p. 8). "The so-called *Gospel according to the Hebrews* was an Aramaic book the existence of which is attested from the middle of the second century," and on p 261 "The Nazarenes who kept true to their mother speech, had from A. D. 150 at the latest, their gospel according to the Hebrews" In his *History of the Canon*, II p 722, after summing up the evidence and speaking of the period about A D 130-150, he says, "To this time the origin of the Gospel according to the Hebrews belongs" For these references I am indebted to the kindness of Dr B B Warfield

[2] See Dr. B. Weiss' Manual of Introd. to N. T , Vol II § 45, 5

[3] It is hardly necessary even to mention the little known *Gospel acc to the Egyptians* a Gnostic document, but one by no means generally accepted by the Gnostics themselves, and distinctly repudiated by Clem of Alexandria, who quotes it.

False Lights That Lead Astray

It is instructive to look back over the course through which the Tubingen School has passed to its downfall, leaving so much spiritual wreck and ruin behind it in the overturning of the faith of many, during the past half century. The founder of this school of theological speculation was Ferdinand Christian Baur. Baur was withdrawn from the orthodox position, which his earliest productions indicate that he held, by the powerful influence of Schleiermacher, and then by that of Strauss, his own pupil, whose "Life of Jesus" seems to have been one of the means by which poor George Eliot was robbed of her faith. But the chief influence which drew him aside was Hegel's philosophy. We need not examine at length the course of his reasoning. Little more is necessary than the mention of his conclusions about the time when the different books of the New Testament were written. He held that Paul wrote the four epistles, to the Romans, Corinthians and Galatians, and that John, the beloved disciple, wrote the Apocalypse; but that the other books of the New Testament are spurious productions, and especially that the four gospels containing the facts which are the basis of Christianity were written long after their reputed authors,

Matthew, Mark, Luke and John, were dead; and that they, therefore, could not have been written by them This conclusion was founded, not upon facts, but upon *a priori* theories. Taking the opposite course from that of the Baconian method of deducing general conclusions from an induction of particular facts, he assumed certain general conclusions as true, and then proceeded to gather and arrange facts in the endeavor to sustain these conclusions. Assuming the impossibility of miracles, and of the supernatural in all its phases, and then adopting the Hegelian theory of the progress of every set of opinions, as going through the three stages of affirmation, contradiction and reconciliation (thesis, anti-thesis, and synthesis), he endeavored to account for the origin of the Christian Scriptures by supposing that they developed in a merely natural way by this rule.

The process, however, is of small importance. What we are concerned with is his conclusions as to the dates of these books, and especially of the four gospels. Placing these four epistles of Paul in this period of "affirmation," he pronounced them genuine and their traditional dates substantially correct. But, according to his theory, the so-called Synoptic Gospels,

Matthew, Mark and Luke, must have originated in the second period—that of discussion and difference. So he concluded that while Matthew may have been written about A. D. 130, in the interest of the Judaizing party, and Luke about 150 in advocacy of universality, Mark could not have originated earlier than the decade from 150 to 160, and that John must have been written in the period of "synthesis" or reconciliation of opposing parties, in the decade extending from A. D. 160 to 170.

III. "SUPERNATURAL RELIGION"

Now, it would not have been necessary to detain the reader with the mention of these opinions of Baur if they had been held by him alone; but this was by no means the case. His views spread rapidly among German scholars, and the very influential Tubingen School was the result. Baur died in 1860, and his influence has long since waned in Germany, as its radical unsoundness has been demonstrated, not only by reasoning, but by unexpected events. But, as its sun was going down in Germany, it was rising on England. About twenty-five years ago there appeared in England a book dealing with these questions in an apparently learned way under the title of *Supernatural Religion.*

The aim of the book was to destroy belief in the supernatural, and especially to discredit the four gospels. It was a popular presentation in English of the Tubingen theories of Baur and his school. The author withheld his name and seems never to have revealed it, though a prominent English review writer has been suspected of the authorship.[1] The book was ushered in with a chorus of praise from reviews, extolling its great learning and fairness in discussion. It was at a time when the Darwinian theories were most zealously propagated, and a large proportion of the most cultivated Englishmen were under the spell of the skepticism which accompanied the reception of these theories. The result was that the book had an enormous sale, passing rapidly from one edition to another, and influenced a very large number of writers and readers in such a way as to lead them, at least, to question the divine origin of the Christian religion and the sacred character of the Holy Scriptures. One thing which, without doubt, added

---

[1] It is now well known that Mr Walter R Cassells is the author of this book, a new edition of which has just appeared

False Lights That Lead Astray 15

greatly to the popularity of this book with its skeptical readers was the fact that it, somehow, came to be understood that the anonymous author was one of the most eminent prelates of the Church of England; a man noted for his profound and accurate scholarship and unswerving faithfulness to his sacred duties during a long life of usefulness. Whether this fiction was given out by the unknown author or by some literary Mephistopheles among his admirers will probably never be known. But the result may, perhaps, be better imagined than described. This more than "dash of heresy" in the supposed production of a bishop long venerated for his learning and piety, gave the dish a piquancy whose charm was irresistible to the palate of the skeptical public, ready at all times, and more than ready at that time, of the beginning of the Darwinian ascendancy, to break away from all the old restraints of religion The fact that a man of such character, standing and ability, who had so long been one of the Church's guides and defenders, had now, as it seemed, joined the sappers and miners who were trying to destroy her foundations, and that this whilom eminent defender, had, in this work, set off a blast which made the whole edifice tremble, filled the free-thinking literati with an excitement from whose intoxication they have hardly yet recovered. The sadly wronged prelate did indeed most emphatically disclaim the authorship, but this seemed of no avail. The book is said to have passed through six editions in as many months. This is probably an exaggeration; but the fact that the assertion is made is an indication that the circulation of the book must have been rapid beyond precedent in the case of a work devoted to learned argument on such a subject.

The book which was lauded by four reviews for its fairness and directness in argument was very soon found, on examination by competent scholars, to conceal, under the guise of vaunted fairness, almost every kind of indirection and unfair dealing. Dr. Lightfoot (afterwards Bishop of Durham) convicted the author of so misrepresenting and warping the facts with which he dealt as to show an unmistakably dishonest intention to "make the worse the better reason seem." The utter misrepresentation of the meaning of authorities quoted, whether made from ignorance or design, indicated a prejudice against the Christian religion which made the author blind to whatever was evidential of its truth and lynx-eyed to the

False Lights That Lead Astray 17

minutest fact that could be construed as unfavorable to it. Dr. Sanday, of Oxford, showed so conclusively the fallaciousness of the writer's argument designed to prove that the Gospel of Luke was derived from the mutilated gospel which Marcion used in propagating his heresy, that he was forced to acknowledge that the Gospel of Luke was the original which, on the other hand, Marcion trimmed and treated to make it appear to support his heresy.

Dr. Lightfoot, in a remarkable set of articles in the *Contemporary Review*, proved that the supposedly learned and fair author of *Supernatural Religion*, either from the lack of even a schoolboy knowledge of Greek, or from design, mistranslated passage after passage, from Irenæus especially, so as to make it appear that the author intended to teach exactly the reverse of that which, on a proper translation and construction of his words, was shown to be his real meaning.

II.

NEW LIGHT ON A MARTYR'S TESTIMONY

I. TATIAN'S DIATESSARON

THE main position around which this great battle raged was *The Diatessaron* of Tatian.

The author of *Supernatural Religion* ventured to assert that "No one seems to have seen Tatian's *Harmony*, probably for the reason that there was no such work" Could he have foreknown the events of the near future, he would have withheld this sarcasm.

During the very next year, 1876, there appeared a translation of Ephræm's Commentary on Tatian's *Diatessaron*, made at the request of the Mechitarist Fathers of San Lazzaro, Venice, by Dr Georgius Moesinger, of the University of Salzburg[1] The author of *Supernatural Religion*, in spite of this, which was a very clear proof of the existence of Tatian's *Harmony*, said in desperation: "It is obvious that there is no evidence of any

[1] This translation was based on an earlier Latin version of the Mechitarist monk, Aucher

value connecting Tatian's gospel with those of our canon."

This he did in 1879, and he most certainly would not have said it if he could have foreseen what was to occur two years later. In 1881 Professor Zahn, of Erlangen, published a reconstruction of the *Diatessaron of Tatian* from Moesinger's translation of the commentary on it, and from the *Homilies of Aphraates* which were, also, based upon it. This made it clear that the *Diatessaron* was not another of the Apocryphal gospels, nor a reproduction of the *Gospel according to the Hebrews*, as had been conjectured, but was a harmony made up of our four gospels

This work of Zahn drew attention to an Arabic manuscript marked No. XIV, in the Vatican library, which purported to contain a translation of the *Diatessaron* itself.

Ciasca, a "lector" of the library, was urged to translate this manuscript and publish it, but was delayed by other duties in doing so, and this providential delay was overruled, like many another, for the best result in the end. There was in the library one day an ecclesiastic, the Visitor Apostolic of the Catholic Copts in Egypt. He was invited to examine the manuscript, and as a result, informed

Ciasca that he knew of another like it in Egypt, and that he would have it sent to him. In due time this was done, and thus Ciasca had two Arabic copies from which to make his translation. He completed and published his translation in 1888, in time to present it to the Pope on the occasion of his jubilee in that year. Now we have it in English in a translation with notes by the Rev. Hope W. Hogg, B. D., and his wife, who gave him much assistance in the undertaking, as well as an earlier by B. Hamlyn Hill, B. D., called *The Earliest Life of Christ.*

Two facts make it of great importance as a witness for the four gospels. One is that it contains the whole account given of our Saviour's life and teachings in the gospels, in the very words of the gospels, woven together so as to make a continuous narrative, and is therefore appropriately named the *Diatessaron*, *i. e*, through four.

The second fact is that there is no trace of any Apocryphal gospel in it, showing that the only gospels recognized by the Christians of that early day, fifty or sixty years after the death of the last of the apostles, were those of Matthew, Mark, Luke, and John. The preparation of a life of our Saviour out of these gospels, and these alone, without a word of his own (as Ebed Jesu puts it, "and of his own he did not add a single saying") indicates the universal acceptance of these gospels long before, as well as the reverential awe entertained of them as "The memoirs of the apostles," as Tatian's teacher, Justin Martyr, called them. This is too evident to need amplification or argument.

The *Diatessaron*, according to the careful estimate made by Prof. G. F. Moore, contains fifty per cent of Mark, sixty-six per cent of Luke, 76.5 per cent of Matthew and ninety-six per cent of John. Before the discovery of the *Diatessaron*, the Rev. W. M. Taylor, D. D., of New York, composed a harmony of the same character, which he named *The Life of Our Lord in the Words of the Four Evangelists*, a book which was constantly used for daily reading by one whose memory is more precious to the writer than that of any other human being; and it would be as irrational to deny that Dr. Taylor[1] had our four gospels before him when he arranged that harmony, as to say that Tatian did not have them when he wove them together to make his. Duplicate expressions and narratives in

[1] Dr. Taylor omits the genealogies, just as Tatian does.

the different gospels were, of course, omitted by both in a work of such a character.

The composition of the *Diatessaron* implies that the four gospels were the *only* gospels of the Christians for a long time before it came into existence, in spite of the efforts of Basilides, Marcion, and other heretics to corrupt or supplant them.

But an interesting question is, are there traces of the existence of these gospels during the period which lies between the death of John and the composition of the *Diatessaron*? This period, as every student of church history is aware, lies in great obscurity. Whether from the destruction of libraries, the prevalence of persecution or whatever cause, the distinct Christian memorials of that time are few. Indeed this may be said of the time from the close of The Acts of the Apostles to the death of the Apostle John, also. Yet there are lights here and there in this dark morass where the paths are so indistinct and our footing so uncertain. I need not speak of the clear evidence of the existence of the four gospels and other books of the New Testament furnished by the fragments of the writings of apostolic fathers which have been preserved to our time. For these testimonies the reader will turn to such text-books on Christian evidences as that of Paley, or to the much fuller and fresher presentation of them in the almost phenomenal production of the great German scholar, Dr. Bernhardt Weiss, *Manual of Introduction to the New Testament:*[1] or to the still better and sounder presentation in Charteris's *Canonicity.*

But in addition to the references to these writings in the scanty Christian literature which has survived from the apostolic age to our own, we have the account of a thoroughly reliable writer, who lived from about twenty years after the death of the Apostle John to the opening of the third century, of oral communications which he had received from one who was a disciple of John himself, and was accustomed to talk with others who had seen the Lord; and he tells us that these communications by word of mouth agreed with the accounts of Christ given in the gospels. This testimony of Irenæus is contained in a letter to a friend of his youth, who with him had been a hearer of Polycarp, the younger contemporary of the Apostle John, but who seems

---

[1] As remarkable, however, for the lameness and impotency of some of its conclusions as it is for its evidence of scholarship and diligent research

to have fallen away from the simplicity of the gospel under the influence of political ambitions and heathen philosophy. Writing to this former companion, Florinus, Irenæus says:—

"I distinctly remember the incidents of that time better than events of recent occurrence; for, the lessons received in childhood, growing with the soul, become identified with it; so that I can describe the very place in which the blessed Polycarp used to sit when he discoursed, and his goings out and his comings in, and his manner of life, and his personal appearance, and the discourses which he held before the people, and how he would describe his intercourse with John, and with the rest who had seen the Lord, and how *he would relate their words*. And whatsoever things he had heard from them about the Lord, and about his miracles, and about his teaching, Polycarp, as having received them from eyewitnesses of the life of the word, *would relate altogether in accordance with the Scriptures*"

Of this, Dr. Wace (*The Authenticity of the Four Gospels*) remarks:—

"In order to appreciate what this involves, one must ask what Irenæus meant by 'The

Scriptures.' Of course, the expression must refer to those portions of the Scriptures which narrate the life of our Lord, and Irenæus has stated, in a memorable passage, what these records were. In the third book of his great work on *The Refutation and Overthrow of Knowledge Falsely so Called*, he relates briefly, says Bishop Lightfoot: 'The circumstances under which the four gospels were written. . . . He assumes throughout, not only that our four canonical gospels alone were acknowledged in the church in his own time, but that this had been so from the beginning.'"

Irenæus, who quotes our four gospels 500 times in those of his writings which have been preserved, and the Gospel of John 100 times, was a contemporary, for perhaps thirty-five years, of Polycarp, whose memory as his teacher he ever held in most affectionate reverence. Polycarp was the contemporary of the Apostle John for thirty years at the least. Irenæus regarded the four gospels just as the orthodox Christian of our day does. Now, Irenæus has much to say of Justin and his child in the gospel, Tatian. They lived for thirty years in one case, and perhaps forty in the other as his contemporaries. Tatian and Justin were contemporaries of Polycarp for the first forty or forty-five years of their lives.[1] The *Diatessaron* of Tatian frees the testimony of Justin Martyr of all possible doubt, and to that testimony our attention will now be directed. The *Diatessaron* has been well-named "the key to Justin."

II. JUSTIN, THE APOLOGIST AND MARTYR

Somewhere about the time when the Apostle John died at Ephesus, there was born at the village of Sychar, by Jacob's well, where our Saviour told the Samaritan woman of the water of life, a child who was to be known through all coming ages as a martyr for his cause. But, Justin Martyr, though a native of Sychar, was not of Samaritan blood. Had we no information to the contrary, we should be likely to think that he was probably a descendant of some one of those with whom our Lord spent two days on his journey northward

---

[1] "Polycarp was eighty-six years old at the time of his death (from his words it would seem that he had been eighty-six years a Christian) and Irenæus speaks of him as a disciple of John, and as appointed Bishop of Smyrna by apostles, and again speaks of 'successors of Polycarp at the present time,' that is, from A D 177 to A D 190 .
Living from A D 70 to 155, his life and work link together St John and Irenæus, and they become an argument for the authenticity of the Fourth Gospel, the force of which it is impossible to deny "—*Watkins' Bampton Lectures*, pp 391, 2

—two days of surpassing interest they must have been—when, after hearing his wonderful words, they said to the woman of Samaria: "Now we believe, not because of thy saying for we have heard him ourselves, and know that this is indeed the Christ." But it is evident from all that he says that he was not of Samaritan or of Jewish blood, and that he was reared in the study of philosophy and Greek literature, and without any knowledge of the Old Testament. Philosophy was his pursuit from his youth, and he early won the right to wear the philosopher's cloak. He seems to have been in the habit of retiring to some solitude to do what almost every great thinker has done—meditate, and commune with nature. It was such an excursion that was made, in God's providence, the occasion of his coming to the knowledge of the truth. The place was probably in the vicinity of Ephesus, as he seems to have studied there; but this is immaterial. Let us hear him tell of it: "And while I was thus disposed, when I wished at one period to be filled with great quietness, and to shun the path of men, I used to go into a certain field not far from the sea, and when I was near that spot one day, which having reached, I proposed to be by myself, a certain old man, by no means contemptible in appearance, exhibiting meek and venerable manners, followed me at a little distance."

After salutations, the venerable stranger told Justin that he had come to this place to look for friends who were absent and who might be returning. As it was in view of the sea, he was probably looking for the vessel by which they were expected.

Justin having told him that he delighted in solitary walks to meditate on the great questions of philosophy, the stranger began to discourse of the vanity of mere human speculations about the great subject of religion (for this was the field of philosophy in which Justin was most interested), and then dwelt on the need of a divine revelation such as existed in The Prophets, or Old Testament Scriptures, and of the enlightenment of the Holy Spirit, to give us a satisfactory and saving view of the truth in these great matters. Then, Justin tells us:—

"When he had spoken these and many other things, he went away, bidding me attend to them, and I have not seen him since; but straightway a flame was kindled in my soul, and a love of the prophets and of those men who are the friends of Christ possessed me, and whilst revolving his words in my mind, I found this philosophy alone to be safe and profitable." (Dialogue Ch. 8.)[1]

Thus we see how it was that Justin Martyr, though he became a Christian, never ceased to wear his philosopher's cloak. He found Christianity to be the truest and highest of all philosophy, and did not cease to be a philosopher by becoming a Christian.[2] He seems to have been one of the most fearless and straightforward of all the witnesses for Christ in that brave age. Anyone who will read his two defenses of Christianity will see and feel this as he cannot otherwise do.

Some years later, probably in 163, there was a thrilling scene in the court of the Roman prefect, Rusticus. The noble life was crowned with the noblest of deaths, that of a martyr for Christ.

---

[1] Justin seems to have been influenced, too, as we know Calvin was, by the conduct of those whom he observed under persecution. He tells us: "While I still found delight in the doctrines of Plato, and heard the Christians calumniated, but yet saw them fearless toward death, and all that men account fearful, I learned that it was impossible that they should live in sin and lust"

[2] "The torch of Aristotle and Plato faded when he became familiar with the light of Christ"—*Watkins' Bampton Lectures.*

Hart and Volkmar date the first *Apology* A D 145–148, Caspari and Kruger earlier.—*Watkins' Bampton Lectures.*

Rusticus, the prefect of Rome, before whom Justin and other Christians were arraigned, demanded that they should deny their faith and salute the image of the emperor as divine. "Unless," said he, "ye obey, ye shall be mercilessly punished." Justin said, "Through prayer we can be saved on account of our Lord Jesus Christ, even when we have been punished, because this shall become to us salvation and confidence at the more awful judgment seat of our Lord and Saviour." Thus also said the other martyrs: "Do what you will, for we are Christians and do not sacrifice to idols."

Thus, like Moses, they endured, as "seeing him who is invisible."

III. JUSTIN AS A WITNESS

Let us now turn to the utterances of Justin Martyr addressed, in his two *Apologies*, to Antoninus Pius, the emperor of Rome.

Dr. Basil Gildersleeve in the introduction to his edition of Justin's *Apologies*, says:—

"If Justin was acquainted with the Fourth Gospel, the whole fabric of a great historical school falls to the ground."

This must be clear to all; for if the first *Apology* was not written till as late as A. D., 147 the date which Professor Gildersleeve favors, it was written several years before the date assigned to the Gospel of John by the Tubingen School, *i. e*, A. D 160–170. Neander thinks the first *Apology* should be dated A. D. 139. He says: "After the death of the Emperor Hadrian, persecutions arose against the Christians, in the beginning of the reign of Antoninus Pius. Thereby Justin, who was then resident at Rome, was induced to address a writing in defense of the interests of the Christians to the emperor. Since, however, in the superscription of this work, *he does not give the title of Cæsar to M. Aurelius*, it is probably to be inferred that it was written before his adoption into that dignity, which took place in A. D. 139"

But, taking the late date, there can be no doubt that Justin quotes it, and he surely could not have quoted it from thirteen to twenty-three years before it was written, or one minute before it was written, for that matter.

That Justin did know John's Gospel, must be clear to any open-minded person who will read in his first *Apology*, chapter sixty-one, these words:—

"Except ye be born again, ye cannot enter into the kingdom of heaven." In addition to this he goes on to mention other words spoken in this conversation of Christ with Nicodemus, recorded in the third chapter of John's Gospel.

In his dialogue with Trypho, chapter ninety-one, we find Justin giving a comment on John 3:14, and several times he refers to the name which John gives to Christ—the Logos—"the word."[1] It seems plain enough then that Justin, the successor of Aristides and Quadratus as a defender of the faith did have the Gospel of John in his hands, and therefore, "the whole fabric of a great historical school falls to the ground." Baur may hold the theory according to which the Gospel of John could not have been written till from A. D. 160 to 170; but we find as a fact that it is quoted by Justin in his *Apology* addressed to the Emperor Antoninus Pius, and the theory must yield to the fact, and "fall to the ground." How is it with the three synoptic gospels?

See how Justin speaks of all the gospels together under a name which may be unfamiliar to some of us, but which seems a very natural designation for them. He draws, in a few words, a picture of the worship of the Christians on Sunday. He tells the emperor:

[1] Not in Philo's sense.—*Gildersleeve.*

"On the day called the day of the Sun (Sunday)[1] there is a gathering together of all who dwell in city and country, with one accord (or in one place), and the *Memoirs of the Apostles* and the writings of the prophets are read." He continues with a further description of their worship including the administration of the Lord's Supper. The significant thing for us here is that *The Memoirs of the Apostles* are read in public worship and are evidently regarded as sacred scriptures, as they are read along with Old Testament Scriptures. But a question has been raised as to whether these *Memoirs of the Apostles* were our gospels, which contain apostolic memoirs of our blessed Lord. The controversy has been an earnest and prolonged one; but it is hard to see how there can be any room for a difference of opinion about the matter. We need not go outside of the writings of Justin himself to determine without a shadow of doubt about what were the Memoirs of the Apostles. We need only cast our eyes up to the preceding chapter of the first apology on the same page (first Apology chapter sixty-six) and we read "The apostles in the memoirs

---

[1] τῇ τοῦ ἡλίου λεγομένῃ ἡμέρα.

drawn up by them, which are called gospels,[1] thus enjoined on them, that Jesus taking bread, having blessed it, said, 'This do in remembrance of me; this is my body, and taking the cup, and having given thanks, said, This is my blood,'" etc.

Surely this is conclusive as to what the *Memoirs of the Apostles* are. Justin calls them "gospels," and we find in them what we find to-day in our gospels. Now if there could be any lingering doubt that this general name—*Memoirs of the Apostles*—means our four gospels, we may turn to another work of Justin where it is used and see proofs which must immediately scatter these doubts to the winds. In the Dialogue with Trypho, chapter one hundred, we read: "But also in the gospel it is written 'All things are delivered me of my Father,' and 'No man knoweth the Father but the Son; nor the Son but the Father, and they to whom the Son will reveal him.'" We know,

---

[1] Hostile critics have alleged that this last expression is an interpolation. But, there is no manuscript evidence to support this allegation, and the only reason they have made it seems to be that the words are so plainly fatal to their contention. The text is, so far as is known, as sound here as elsewhere. "When a manuscript is found that does not contain the words 'which are called gospels,' the gloss theory will deserve respect. Till then it has not a rag of reason to hide its nakedness."—Nicholson on *the Gospel according to the Hebrews*, p 134.

New Light on a Martyr's Testimony 35

of course, that this is from our Gospel of Matthew 11:27, and so, what Justin states is written in the gospel,[1] we find in our Gospel of Matthew. But he continues: "Christ called one of his disciples, previously known as Simon, Peter, since he recognized him to be the Christ, the Son of God, by the revelation of his Father; and since we find it recorded in the *Memoirs of the Apostles*," etc. All will recognize this as from the sixteenth chapter of Matthew, and this he says is "recorded in the *Memoirs of the Apostles*." So our Matthew must be a part of these *Memoirs of the Apostles*. Look on a little farther, and in chapter 103 we read:—

"For, if the Memoirs which I say were drawn up by the apostles and those who followed them, it is recorded that his sweat fell down like blood while he was praying and saying, if it be possible let this cup pass," etc.

Here we find a quotation combining Luke 22:41 and 42, and Matthew 26:39 and he speaks of it as being "recorded in the Memoirs

---

[1] "Gospel" is often used to mean the four gospels, as Watkins puts it, "to express the unity of a collected plurality." Justin so uses it.—See *Watkins' Bampton Lectures*.

See, also, Charteris's *Canonicity*, especially p 63, footnote

which were drawn up by the apostles, and those who followed them." Now, Matthew and John whom he quoted were apostles and Mark and Luke were their followers,—Mark of Peter and Luke of Paul, for he quotes both of these extensively also.

If we had space, I should like to transcribe the fifteenth chapter of the first *Apology*, and show how, in it he quotes, Matthew seven times, Mark eight times, and Luke five times, so that in the short chapter of less than two 12mo pages we have a cluster of selections from the three synoptic gospels with only a few words of his own to serve as a thread to hold together the jewels gathered from these "*Memoirs of the Apostles.*"[1] I think we would be very unreasonable to demand plainer proof that Justin Martyr had just the gospels we have and no others—and refers to them as *Memoirs of the Apostles.*

Prof. James Drummond, Unitarian critic, and follower of Martineau, says of the foolish charge that John was copied from Justin:[2]—

"It does seem to me surprising that any one in comparing the passages in Justin and John

[1] See Appendix
[2] It is somewhat remarkable that one set of critics find nothing of John's Gospel in Justin, and another set find so much that they make this charge.

should doubt for one moment that the dependence is on the side of the former."

This sufficiently "Liberal" critic concludes: " I must conclude, therefore, as best satisfying, on the whole, the facts of the case, not only that Justin regarded the Fourth Gospel as one of the historical 'memoirs' of Christ, but that it is not improbable that he believed in its Johannean authorship. This is a very old-fashioned conclusion, but I have endeavored simply to follow the evidence without any ulterior object and must leave the result to the judgment of the reader."

How remarkably this "old-fashioned conclusion" for which he felt bound to apologize, has been confirmed by the discovery of *The Diatessaron!* Since this discovery, no self-respecting critic, however great his prejudices, can, if fully informed, either assert the dependence of John's Gospel on Justin or deny that Justin knew our four gospels, and them alone, as the authoritative Christian records of Christ's life and teachings.

It is very hard to see how any honest reader of Justin's *Apologies* and *Dialogue* could have any doubt of this fact, since quotations from the Synoptic Gospels occupy a large proportion of the space these writings cover, and besides evident references to, and quotations from, the Gospel of John, the whole of these writings are permeated with the unique thought of this gospel which stands apart from all that has ever been written by the hand of man.

The destructive critic Thoma, even, says of Justin: "He cites the Synoptics; he thinks and argues according to John."

All this was evident before the discovery of *The Diatessaron.* Now, the case is settled; for we find Tatian, who became a Christian under the instruction of Justin about A. D. 150, making a harmony out of the four gospels, and using ninety-six per cent of the Gospel of John in doing so, only four per cent being omitted because duplicated by statements in the other gospels

"It is certain," says Dr. B. Weiss, "that Justin is also acquainted with Pauline epistles and is influenced by them. It is characteristic throughout that what he has chiefly adopted from the Epistle to the Romans is the application of the Old Testament in the Christian sense, as appears from the many citations common to both in their form, connection and application (comp Rom 3: 11–17 and Dial. 27; 9: 27 ff. and Dial. 55; 11: 16 and Dial. 42;

11: 2 ff. and Dial. 39-46; 14: 11 and Dial. 52), and the repeated statements respecting the justification of Abraham as the father of believing Gentiles, taken from Rom. 4: (Dial. 11; 23-119)."

For proof of Justin's use of other Pauline epistles see Weiss' Introduction §7. 4.

Weiss shows with equal clearness Justin's use of the Fourth Gospel. Lack of space prevents the presentation of the evidence in his words; but his conclusion is that "the opinion that Justin was not yet acquainted with the Fourth Gospel, once so obstinately adhered to by the Tubingen School, must be regarded as definitely set aside."

Justin sometimes quotes the gospels with the formula, "It is written," indicating that he regards them as Scripture.

The use of the Epistle of James (Dial. 1.16), of 1 Peter (Dial. 72), and of The Acts (1 Apology, 39, 40, 50), is clearly shown. His knowledge of The Revelation and the fact that it was written by the Apostle John, is indicated by such words as these:—(Dial. 81).

"There was a certain man with us [Christians] whose name was John, one of the apostles of Christ, who prophesied by a revelation that was made to him." Then follows a reference to the "thousand years, the general, and, in short, eternal resurrection and judgment of all men." Rev. 20.

It is true that Justin does not always use the precise words of our received text. He evidently wrote with a rapidly running pen, and in the case of the second Apology, written, probably, on the eve of his execution, he evidently did not turn to each passage to verify his quotations. He joins together the words of two or three of the gospels in relating an incident or stating a truth. Yet I think no one can point out a single expression which belongs to any of the apocryphal gospels.

The apocryphal "Gospel of Peter," discovered a few years ago at Akhmim in Egypt, which was in all probability the oldest of all the apocryphal gospels, is not quoted once. Justin's quotations are just such as would naturally be made by a man of great earnestness who had his memory well stored with the Scriptures, and had a vast number of quotations at his command, but did not turn to the chapter and verse, and copy every word accurately. We should remember that there were no chapters and verses then, and that Alexander Cruden was not yet born

But, lest any should think me liable to mistake on this point, I will, before concluding, quote the words of Westcott (Canon, p. 151). Says he: "It is enough to repeat in the presence of these facts that differences from the present text of the gospels such as are found in the present text of Justin are wholly inadequate to prove that passages so differing could not have been taken from copies of our gospels." And this was written before the discovery of the apocryphal so-called "Gospel of Peter," and *The Diatessaron* of Tatian.

It is proper to remark that almost certainly there were some differences between the text of the gospels used by Justin and our received text, or that of Westcott and Hort; but the main differences between his quotations and our New Testament are due (as is plainly the case in his Old Testament quotations) to the fact that he quoted freely from memory and not with Bible and concordance in his hands

Dr. Purves has rendered a great service to the cause of truth and sound criticism by his L. P. Stone lectures on Justin Martyr, delivered at Princeton, and no one, unless dominated by prejudice, can rise from the perusal of his fifth lecture, in which he brings a great mass of evidence from the two *Apologies* and the *Dialogue* to show Justin's use of the writings which we now call the New Testament, without agreeing in his conclusion that Justin had "reference to a distinct Christian literature, which, while nothing definite is said of its authority in the Church, was evidently regulative of the Church's faith."

The fact that Justin speaks of the gospels as read in the public worship of Christians along with the writings of the prophets, that he quotes the gospels with the formula, "It is written," together with his reverent use of what he calls "our writings" (—— Scriptures), indicates that, having the New Testament almost, if not quite, in its entirety,[1] he regarded it, though not yet "canonized" by any ecclesiastical council, as invested with the authority of apostles who had received the Holy Spirit according to Christ's promise, and "the promise of the Father."

Referring to the peculiarities of the text which Justin had before him, Dr. Purves says (p. 218):—

---

[1] Dr. Eberhard Nestle, in his work, Introduction to Textual Criticism of the New Testament, though once a professor of Tubingen, moots the question (following Zahn), "Whether the entire New Testament, as the Doctrine of Addai says, was not a present which Tatian brought with him from Rome to his fellow-countrymen," etc

"We do not mean that Justin's text is now represented in its entirety by any one manuscript or class of manuscripts, but that he gives evidence of that corruption of the canonical texts which, according to abundant testimony, took place even in the century immediately succeeding that in which they were written, and which most plainly appears in those manuscripts which textual critics have classified as 'Western.' If, however, this be so, then Justin testifies, not only that our synoptic gospels existed in his day and were used by the Church as public documents, and were regarded as apostolic and authoritative records of the life of Christ; but he also proves, by the incidental character of his quotations and by their very variations from the text of our gospels, that these latter were, in the middle of the second century, already ancient books, handed down from the apostolic age. No more explicit testimony to our synoptic gospels could well be asked of him; and the very difficulties which at first present themselves in his quotations, in the end confirm his evidence for their apostolic authority."

Farther on (p. 248) he declares, "It is clear that at least the gospels had been formed into a sacred collection called 'the gospel' which ranked on an equality with the Old Testament, and that other apostolic books were used to regulate the faith of the Church"

The strange mistake of Eusebius in interpreting the words of Papias seems to be responsible for the figment of a second John,[1] and so to have helped to fashion one feature of that persistent ghost, the "Johannean problem," though Eusebius himself had not a shadow of a doubt that the Fourth Gospel was written by the Apostle John.

It is to be hoped that the phantom of false authorship, at least, is laid now, since Tatian's *Diatessaron* has risen from the dust of long oblivion to show unmistakably that Tatian's teacher, Justin, had the gospel of that John whom Justin describes as "one of the disciples of Christ," and the writer of The Revelation.[2]

---

[1] See Farrar's Early Days of Christianity Appendix, Excursus XIV I think that no unprejudiced person who understands Greek can read this "Excursus" without being convinced that Eusebius misunderstood Papias. John the Presbyter was John the Apostle The fact that there are two tombs of Washington at Mt Vernon does not prove that there were two Washingtons, and the fact that there were two tombs at Ephesus, each claimed to be a tomb of John, does not prove that there were two Johns

[2] Origen says, (Commentary on John, Book I, Chap. 6), "The gospels then, being four, I deem the firstfruits of the gospels to be that which you have enjoined me to search into according to my powers the Gospel of John"

Again, he says, "But Luke, though he says at the begin-

This new light on the old monument has made its inscriptions clear to all—but the blind.

In the presence of evidence so incontrovertible, it is a strange thing to find a professor in a Congregational Theological Seminary speaking, in a late work,[1] of the Gospel of John as "a writing about the middle of the second century." But then, when we find that this theological professor does not believe in Christ, except as a mere man, and remember how clearly the Gospel of John teaches his divinity, we see the explanation. Something had to be done to get this gospel out of the way; and so in the face of all the overwhelming evidence of the falsity of the Tübingen theory, he still adheres to it.

It may be true that German theological theories " go to England when they die," but they do not stop there. America is receiving

ning of The Acts 'The former treatise did I make about all that Jesus began to do and teach,' yet leaves to him who lay on Jesus' breast the greatest and completest discourses about Jesus "

There was no "Johannean problem" to Origen, and it may be safely asserted that no man living from A D 185 to the middle of the third century knew every scrap of early Christian literature so thoroughly as he

[1] Evolution of Trinitarianism, Professor Paine, Bangor Theol Sem

a full share of these unquiet and disquieting spirits to haunt her halls of theological learning, while their carcasses still pollute the religious atmosphere of Germany.

III.

THE GREAT LIGHT FROM THE VATICAN

1. THE reader will naturally wish to know more of the *Diatessaron* of Tatian, Justin's pupil, which, in God's good providence, arose from its long sleep and showed so plainly that Justin had our four gospels and no others.

When Ciasca showed Antonius Morcos, the Apostolic Visitor of the Catholic Copts, the Arabic copy of the *Diatessaron* in the Vatican library, this ecclesiastic, as we have seen, promised to send him another manuscript of the same work which was owned by a gentleman in Egypt. So there are now in Rome two Arabic copies of the *Diatessaron*. The Egyptian manuscript bears upon it the name of the donor in the following inscription at the end: "A present from Halīm Dōs Ghālī, the Copt, the Catholic, to the Apostolic See, in the year of Christ, 1886."

This codex is described as follows: "The codex consists of three hundred and fifty-three leaves. There is no date attached, but the manuscript seems to belong, at the latest, to the fourteenth century. The pages are nine by six and one-quarter inches, inclosed in an illuminated square of golden, red and purple lines, with an ornamentation of golden asterisks."[1]

This manuscript was of great service in supplying two lacunæ in the first, caused by the loss of two folios, and in determining doubtful readings. It is described as being better than the first, in text and other respects, but quite inferior to it in orthography.

It was deposited in the Borgian Library, and, from this fact, has been named the Borgian manuscript, while the other is called the Vatican, because it has long been, and still is, in the Vatican library. It is entirely clear that these manuscripts are not copied the one from the other, nor from any common exemplar, though they have a common Syriac remote ancestor.

In speaking of the great interest excited by the discovery of the "New Syriac Gospels," by Mrs. Lewis, in 1892, Prof. Rendel Harris says, that "one of the first questions that will be asked will be, 'Why have you not done it into English?'" This has, at last, been done

[1] For fuller account see articles by Prof M Maher in *The Month*, London, for November and December, 1892.

The Great Light from the Vatican 49

in the case of Tatian's great work, and we have *The Diatessaron done into English.* We now have it in the recently published ninth volume of *The Ante-Nicene Fathers*, translated, according to the statement of the titlepage, by Rev. Hope W. Hogg, B. D., though he informs us that his wife translated the larger part for him. The statement of the title-page is, then, made on the principle, *Qui facit per alium facit per se*, only the *alium* should be *aliam* in this case.

It is in keeping with a great trend of our times that we find the Cambridge ladies, Mrs. Lewis and her sister Mrs Gibson, going to the St. Catherine Convent at Mount Sinai, and discovering the Syriac Gospels, and then see this Oxford lady working side by side with her husband in giving the *Diatessaron* of Tatian to the English-speaking world.

But an interesting question is, what of the form and contents of the *Diatessaron?*

II. THE DIATESSARON AS WE NOW HAVE IT

Harmonies are made in two forms, either in parallel columns (where the subject is mentioned by more than one evangelist), or with all the gospels interwoven, so as to give a continuous narrative of events and utterances. The *Diatessaron*, or Harmony, of Tatian is of the latter kind.

(a) *A Continuous Account*

The narratives of all the evangelists are combined so as to give an account of our Saviour's life and teachings in chronological order, so far as the compiler could determine this order. In this respect it is like the late Dr. William M. Taylor's *Life of Our Lord in the Words of the Four Evangelists*, and other harmonies which might be mentioned. Hence, some old writers speak of it as the "gospel of the *combined*," as distinguished from the *distinct* gospels.

(b) *The Genealogies Omitted*

Tatian omitted the genealogies. Theodoret intimates that this was due to a heretical tendency, and says that he also omitted everything which indicated that our Saviour was descended from David That the last accusation is due to the prejudice of the heresy hunter is made clear by an inspection of the *Diatessaron*. No such omissions are to be found. On the other hand, in the very first section, Christ is spoken of as the son of David. "The Lord God shall give unto him the throne of his father

David"[1] is the expression which, above all others, would have been omitted in such a case, but it is found here, coupled with the announcement that "he shall be great, and shall be called the Son of the Highest." He did omit the genealogies, but so does Dr. Taylor, who surely will never be accused of Docetism. The omission was evidently due to the fact that it would be difficult to fit them into a continuous narrative.[2]

(c) *The Diatessaron is Divided into Fifty-five Sections*

It is only in comparatively recent times that our Bibles have been divided into chapters and verses for convenience of reference, and it is altogether probable that this division of the *Diatessaron* into sections was made for the convenience of those who read it in public services in Syria for several centuries. The division could not have been made by a man of Tatian's sense. It looks like the work of an idiot in many places, as there is no regard whatever to the subject, the division often coming in the middle of a narrative. Rendel

[1] Luke 1 . 32.
[2] The two Arabic manuscripts, the Vatican and the Borgian, have the genealogies, the first side by side in the narrative, and the latter appended at the close. They have evidently been added by another hand after Tatian's day

Harris suggests that this division into fifty-five sections was made in order that the whole might be read in churches[1] during the year on the Sabbaths and principal feasts. This seems altogether probable; but it is time to look at —

(d) *Some Peculiar Readings of the Diatessaron*

We should remember that it was almost inevitable that there should be many expressions which would sound rather strange to ears accustomed to the rhythm of the familiar words of King James' version, which we have heard from our childhood. Even the Revised Version sometimes at first surprised us with an unfamiliar expression, though that is professedly not a new translation, but a revision of that of King James'. The *Diatessaron* was, as far as we can trace it, a Syriac Version. On the other hand, *we* have had the Greek text of the New Testament, the nearest to the original that could be determined by all the critical means available, and from it our English version was made, and the revised version was based chiefly on the Greek text of Westcott and Hort, the

---

[1] This is another reason for the omission of the genealogies They may, indeed, have been in the original work; but excluded in the preparation of it for public reading

greater correctness of which was secured through many sources unknown when King James' version was translated.

It is necessary to remember that the *Diatessaron* was almost certainly composed in Syriac. In spite of its Greek name and other reasons which Harnack urged for thinking that it was originally composed in Greek, Syriac scholars who have examined the question with great care pronounce it as certain that it was a Syriac book. At any rate, we know that from the early dawn of Syrian Christianity it was used in the churches in Syria. Therefore, when we read the *Diatessaron* in the English version just published, we are reading the translation of a text that branched off from the Greek very early, and that has passed through many vicissitudes, and may have suffered changes by the mistakes of copyists, by mistranslations in passing from version to version, and that has been influenced, as we have clear evidence, by contact with different versions which are well known. The accretions, and other changes from such sources, are noted by the learned editor of the *Diatessaron* in abundant footnotes. This being so, we need not expect the version before us to tally exactly with either our Authorized or the Revised Version. In spite of all this, it is seldom that the meaning is affected to any marked degree. Some of the most singular turns of expression will be given, though, of course, the space allowed will not admit of any full display of these peculiarities. Here are some examples: —

Old Simeon was preserved till he had "seen with his eyes the Messiah of the Lord." And in this form we have his "*Nunc Dimittis*," "Now loosest thou the bonds of thy servant, O Lord, in peace." We are rather surprised at the expression in the account of the offering of the Magi (which seems natural enough, however, when we remember that the camel was then, as it still is, used to cross the desert), "They opened their saddlebags and offered to him offerings of gold, frankincense, and myrrh" (Matt. 2: 11). In the account of the visit to Jerusalem during our Saviour's childhood, we are told that Joseph and his mother "supposed that he was with the children of their company" (Luke 2: 44)

The version of John 1: 18, giving a glimpse of the inscrutable relations of the Father and Son, is, "the only Son, God, which is in the bosom of the Father, he hath told of him" In that scene in which John pointed out Christ to his own disciples, as John saw Jesus coming unto him, we hear him saying: "This is the lamb of God that taketh on itself the burden of the sins of the world" (John 1: 29). When his family could not understand the change that came over him when he began his public ministry and spoke his wonderful words and did his wonderful deeds, we are told, "And his relatives heard, and went out to take him, and said, He hath gone out of his mind." We find the *Diatessaron* following the Greek more closely and translating it more literally than our own English versions in the account of the thronging of the multitude about him when he was healing many, "so that they were *almost falling upon* ($\dot{\epsilon}\pi\iota\pi\iota\pi\tau\epsilon\iota\nu$) *him*, on account of their seeking to get near him" (Mark 3: 10). The two sparrows are spoken of as "sold for a farthing *in a bond*." The meaningless phrase "in a bond" seems to have crept into the text by the similarity of the Syriac word for "farthing" and that for "in a bond." Indeed, a footnote tells us that the two phrases are but different explanations of the same Syriac consonants. In the account of the giving of sight to the blind man, Bartimæus, we have one of the many indications of the line of descent—the family genealogy, so to speak—of the *Diatessaron* text. When our Saviour asks the blind man what he wishes him to do for him, the *Diatessaron* represents him as replying, "My Lord and Master, that my eyes may be opened, *so that I may see thee*." This remarkable addition to our Greek text is found, like many of the peculiar readings of the *Diatessaron*, in the Curetonian Syriac manuscript. Several of these, too, are found in the "New Syriac Gospels," as Rendel Harris calls them, discovered by Mrs. Lewis at Mt. Sinai in 1892. These peculiar expressions indicate a relationship between the *Diatessaron* and the Curetonian and Lewis texts. But more of this anon. Passing on to the betrayal of our blessed Lord, we find the expression in reference to the thirty pieces of silver, "the thirty pieces of money, the price of the precious one." The seamless robe is thus referred to: "And his tunic was without sewing, from the top woven throughout." Our Saviour's cry from the cross to his Father is given in a strange form: "Yāīl, Yāīli, why hast thou forsaken me?" In a footnote the translator says, "The syllable 'Ya' is, doubtless, the Arabic interjection, 'O!' so that it is 'O God! O my God!'" etc. The centurion who, at the crucifixion, commanded the guard, is called "the officer of the foot-soldiers," and this the editor considers a mistake of the translator into Arabic. It is, perhaps, unnecessary to give more instances of peculiar readings. These, as has been intimated, are such as we might very naturally expect to find in a text which was translated from the Greek at a very early day, and had been retranslated into Arabic, and, of course, recopied a number of times.

We are familiar with the sight of a large snowball rolled on the ground in various directions, with one object after another adhering to it, having been picked up in its course, while, perhaps, a bit of color on its surface here and there shows the kind of soil on which it has been rolled. It is liable to be somewhat thus with the text that has been translated and copied over and over again. Some accretions will stick to it, and it will take the color of the life and habits and modes of speech of the people among whom it is translated or copied, and the peculiarities of versions with which it has come in contact. A remarkable thing about the *Diatessaron*, is that its text is so pure that no doctrine or fact of the New Testament is at all distorted in it;[1] and the characteristic to which attention should be drawn is, that *Tatian gave only the words of the four evangelists.* No word of explanation connects the phrases that are carefully woven together to set forth the wonderful life and words of Christ. No attempted reconciliation of apparent discrepancies is given; and there is nothing answering to the headings of chapters in our English Bible, even. In the words of the last writer who mentions the *Diatessaron* as a work which he knew, before its disappearance, Abd Ischō (or Ebed Jesu), who died early in the fourteenth century, "With all diligence he attended to the utmost degree to the right order of those things which were done and said by the Saviour; of his own he did not add a single saying "[2]

[1] Yet, when read at family prayers its peculiar expressions enchain the attention of young and old, throwing, as they sometimes do, new light on the narrative.

[2] It seems impossible to account for Harnack's charge of freedom in the handling of the gospels by Tatian in making his harmony, unless he considers the very act of making a harmony one of freedom No harmonist from Tatian's day to our own, it may safely be said, ever handled the gospels with more reverence He seemed to refrain, indeed, from putting in one word of his own, even as a connective, or for purposes of reconciliation of accounts or of explanation of obscurities One does not like to think that the exigencies of Harnack's critical creed may have influenced his judgment.

While the *Diatessaron* gathered some accretions, on the other hand we find that it escaped some corruptions that are found in our Greek received text. One such case, at least, and that a notable one, may be seen in the omission of the account of the woman taken in adultery, which, by the almost unanimous consent of critics, is now considered spurious. It crept into the text very early. But it evidently was not considered a part of the Holy Scripture (though it may have been known as a verbal tradition) in the time of Origen. In his commentary on John, just published, in the same volume with the *Diatessaron*, that account (John 7: 53–8: 11) is omitted. The fact that Tatian omits it indicates that he wrote before it had crept into the text. The *Diatessaron*, does, however, include the gloss (as it almost certainly is), about the angel descending and troubling the water in the pool of Bethesda (John 5:3, 4), and this is an indication of the very early introduction into the text of these words, which were probably written as an explanation by some transcriber who lived early enough to know of this as the traditional belief of the Jews about this pool.

When we see so remarkable a work as the *Diatessaron* in which, with great care, the four gospels are interwoven, one supplying what another omits, in order to form a continuous account of the life of our Lord, we are naturally anxious to know what manner of man it was who, little more than a half century after the last gospel was penned, undertook this labor of love. Tatian, like Justin Martyr, who, it seems, led him to Christ, was a heathen philosopher who came to find the truest philosophy in Christianity.

III. Tatian, the First Harmonist

He is the first harmonist of whom anything is known, and it is not at all probable that there *was* one before him. His great zeal for Christianity, as well as his originality and genius, point to him as the probable inventor of this mode of presenting the life of our blessed Lord on earth.

In the introductory note to the Borgian manuscript of the *Diatessaron* he is called "Titianus, the Greek." This is evidently the mistake of a copyist, for he himself tells us in so many words that he was an Assyrian.[1] It is

---

[1] He was probably of Greek parentage, though born in Assyria. Assyria had been incorporated by Trajan in the Roman province of Syria. Hence he is sometimes called a Syrian.

true that he wrote in Greek as well as in Syriac, of which his *Address to the Greeks* (Λόγος πρὸς Ἑλληνας) is witness. He was a student of philosophy in general, but inclined to that of Plato as his own philosophical creed. He was born and reared a heathen, and, in the prosecution of his studies, traveled over many countries that he might study the systems of various nations. When he became acquainted with the Old Testament Scriptures he was impressed with the fact that these "barbaric books," as he at first considered them (as a Greek philosopher of that day very naturally would), were "too old to be compared with the learning of the Greeks, too divine to be put on a level with their erroneous doctrine." It should be remembered that Moses preceded Herodotus, "the father of history," by more than a millennium, and it is not strange that he should have been impressed with the venerable antiquity of the books which "Moses wrote." Fortunately for him the higher critics were not to be born for nearly two millenniums after his time.

The account of his conversion to Christianity is thus given by Neander, who makes a summary of what Tatian himself tells in his *Address to the Greeks* :—

"He was brought up in heathenism, and frequent travels gave him the opportunity of learning the multifarious sorts of heathen worship which at that time were existing together in the Roman empire None among them all could recommend itself to him as reasonable. Not only did he observe how religion was used in them to the service of sin, but even the highly wrought allegorical interpretations of the ancient myths as symbols of a speculative system of natural philosophy could not satisfy him, and it appeared to him a dishonorable proceeding for a man to attach himself to the popular religion who did not partake in the common religious belief, and who saw nothing in its doctrine about the gods but symbols of the elements and powers of nature. The mysteries into which he suffered himself to be initiated appeared to him also, in the same manner, not to correspond to the expectations which they awakened, and the contradictory systems of philosophy offered him no sure grounds of religious faith He was rendered mistrustful of them by the contradiction which he often observed in those who gave themselves out as philosophers, between the seriousness which they exhibited, for the sake of appearances, in their dress, mien, and language, and the levity of their conduct. While he was in this condition he came to the Old Testament, to which his attention was drawn by what he had heard of the high antiquity of these writings in comparison with the Hellenic religions, as might easily be the case with a Syrian He himself says of the impression which the reading of this book made upon him :—

"'These writings found acceptance with me because of the simplicity of their language, the unstudiedness of the writers, the intelligible history of the creation, because of the prediction of the future, because of the wholesomeness of their precepts, and because of the doctrine of the ONE GOD which prevails throughout them'

"The impression which the study of the Old Testament

The Great Light from the Vatican 63

made on him would appear, from this, to have been with him the preparation for a belief in the gospel

"Coming, in this state of mind, to Rome, he was converted to Christianity by Justin, of whom he speaks with great reverence."—*Neander's Church History, p 418, Rose's translation*

Tatian, like his spiritual father, Justin Martyr, retained his philosopher's cloak after he became a Christian, maintaining the position that he did not cease to be a philosopher in embracing Christianity, but rather advanced to that which is the highest and only true philosophy.

So firmly, however, were some of the *principles* of Platonism rooted in his mind that he seems to have been much influenced by them in his views and teachings during the latter part of his life. While Justin lived, however, we have the best testimony that he was free from the fault of teaching that dualism which is laid to his charge in his latter days.

Some time, we know not how long, after the martyrdom of Justin, he became a leader among the Encratites, and, it seems, declaimed against marriage and the drinking of wine as sinful. He also taught that Adam was not saved, deducing this opinion from the assertion of the Scriptures that "In Adam, all die."

Irenæus and Hippolytus speak of Tatian as, at last, a Gnostic, and Valentinian teachings are attributed to him.

These accusations quite probably contain an element of exaggeration as the result of ecclesiastical zeal, as Tatian is said by Irenæus to have " separated from the Church."

Whatever amount of deflection from the truth of Christianity he may have been guilty of, we may be quite sure that it was due to that fruitful source of heresies in all ages—ours being by no means an exception—the adoption of a false philosophy and the endeavor to fit Christianity to the Procrustean bed thus prepared for it. The whole history of Gnosticism is an illustration of this process as followed in the early days of Christianity, and the destructive school of criticism, founded by Baur of Tübingen on the postulates of the Hegelian philosophy, is an object lesson for our times of the folly of assuming the infallibility of some human theory and then trying to square God's word to it. The reverse order of procedure must suggest itself to every one who believes in the infallibility of the Scriptures as a Revelation from God to man, as the only true and safe course

Irenæus tells us (Adv Hæres. Book I, Ch.

xxviii) that as long as Tatian enjoyed the companionship of Justin Martyr, "he expressed no such views, but after his (Justin's) martyrdom, he separated from the Church," and also that he "composed his own peculiar type of doctrine," and that, among other things, "he declared that marriage was nothing but corruption and fornication."

We may well grieve that one who was so earnest in his advocacy of Christianity, and who held himself always in readiness to lay down his life in testimony of his faith, should, in any degree, have turned from the straight line of orthodoxy, and should, at last, have separated himself from the Church; yet we can never be too grateful for the fact that he composed the *Diatessaron* from the very words of the inspired gospels of our Lord, "adding not one of his own."

Much as we may regret the false views into which a false philosophy and a mistaken zeal led him, it is an additional reason for gratitude that this very departure from orthodoxy on Tatian's part makes the evidence of the *Diatessaron* for the genuineness of the gospels more decisive; because this makes it wellnigh certain that he composed the harmony in the earlier part of his Christian career. This will be more fully considered when we come to make an estimate of the value of the evidence furnished by this work.

We will now turn to look at some of the

IV. Foot-prints of the Diatessaron Down the Ages

There are few books that have come down to us through more than seventeen centuries that have left plainer traces along their paths There is ample evidence of the existence of the work from a very early date down to the time of the Nestorian bishop Ebed Jesu (or, as our translator writes it, Abd Ischo), who died in 1308. For more than five centuries it had been lost, or at least had been unrecognized by the learned, when it was translated into Latin by Ciasca in 1888. We have it now in the two Arabic manuscripts which have been mentioned, as well as the commentary on it written by Ephraem Syrus, who died in A. D. 373. This commentary is in two manuscripts in the Armenian language, which have a common remote ancestor, doubtless, but differ enough to show that neither was copied from the other. These Armenian manuscripts contain a commentary following in a remarkable way the same order of events as the complete Arabic manuscripts of the *Diatessaron* which we now have. It has been remarked that while these Arabic manuscripts show the influence on their text of the Peshito version (or Peshitta, as it is now called), the Armenian manuscripts of Ephraem's commentary contain peculiar readings of the Curetonian manuscript and of that which Rendel Harris considers the Curetonian's ancestor, the Lewis Sinaitic Palimpsest;[1] and references and quotations "go to show that the Armenian text stands much more closely related to the original than does the Arabic" (Introd. in IX. Vol. Ante-Nicene Fathers, § 15)

Thus the Armenian manuscripts are another independent witness, not only of the existence, from very early times, of the *Diatessaron*, but of the fact that Ephraem wrote a commentary on it, for they are manuscripts of that commentary itself.

The *Diatessaron* was very extensively used in Syrian churches until the Peshito version (Peshitta) gradually took its place in the fifth century. Even after this it was studied and valued.

Dionysius Bar Salibi, Bishop of Armida (twelfth century), has this to say of it:

[1] Called by Harris, *The New Syriac Gospels*

"Tatian, disciple of Justin, the philosopher and martyr, selected from the four gospels and combined and composed a gospel, and called it *Diatessaron—i. e*, The Combined, . . . and upon this gospel Mar Ephraem commented. Its commencement was 'In the beginning was the Word.'"

But this, with the exception of the assertion that the *Diatessaron* began with the first verse of the Gospel of John, was said, about 350 years earlier, by a Syriac commentator on the New Testament, Isho 'dad of Merv (A. D. 852), who mentions, also, another *Diatessaron* by Ammonius,[1] who lived nearly a century after Tatian.

As belonging to this (ninth) century, the subscription of the Borgian manuscript should be noted. As we have seen, that states that it was translated from Syriac into Arabic "from an exemplar written by 'Isa-ibn-'Alial-Motatabbib, pupil of Honain ibn-Ishak," who, we learn, was a famous Arabic physician and teacher of Bagdad (d. 773), whose school produced many translators.

---

[1] This Harmony of Ammonius of Alexandria (not Ammonius Saccas) was unlike the *Diatessaron* of Tatian. It was not "combined" or interwoven, but had the four gospels, it would seem, in four parallel columns

Of Isho 'dad of Merv, Prof. Rendel Harris tells us that he transferred to his pages "some of the most astonishing interpretations which are found in Ephraem's commentary, and gives his express statement of his dependence, in these peculiar interpretations, upon the Syrian father." He also tells us that what is true of Isho 'dad is equally true of Bar Salibi and Bar Hebræus,[1] and taking one passage, Matt. 2: 23, as an instance, says:—

' Syriac authors steadily quote, and some of them ascribe to Ephraem, a curious scholium on Matt 2.23" (it is an explanation given by Ephraem of the words, He shall be called a Nazarene), " and this scholium is actually found in the Armenian Commentary."

Victor of Capua, too, had Tatian's *Diatessaron* in A. D. 545. A century earlier, we find Theodoret, the zealous bishop of Cyrrhus, very much exercised over the general use of the *Diatessaron* in the churches of his diocese, and, impressed with the fact that Tatian was a heretic, employing very energetic measures to keep his flock from using it. Writing on Heresies, 453, he says, "I myself found more

[1] Bar Hebræus lived eighty or ninety years after Bar Salibi.

than two hundred copies in reverential use in the churches of our district. All these I collected and removed, replacing them by the gospels of the four Evangelists."

About a century before this, Ephraem, "the most renowned father of the Eastern Church," wrote his commentary, a translation of which from Armenian into Latin was made by Moesinger, as we have seen, in 1876, and texts from which, published by Zahn in 1881, led to the examination and translation of the Arabic manuscript of the *Diatessaron* in the Vatican library, and its publication by Ciasca in time for the Pope's jubilee in 1888.

Another step brings us to Eusebius, and though he does not seem to have been very familiar with the *Diatessaron*, as was natural, he being a writer in Greek and that being in Syriac, yet he speaks of it distinctly and indicates clearly his knowledge of its plan and contents. He says:—

' Tatian having put together a certain harmony ($\sigma \upsilon \nu \acute{\alpha} \varphi \varepsilon \iota \alpha \nu$) and combination (I know not how) of the gospels, named this the Dia Tessaron" ($\Delta \iota \acute{\alpha}\ T \varepsilon \sigma \sigma \acute{\alpha} \rho \omega \nu$). (H E. IV. 29.)

Then, when we go back through a century to Hippolytus, we find him speaking of Tatian as an Encratite and Gnostic.

The Great Light from the Vatican

When we go still farther back to Irenæus, the teacher of Hippolytus, we find him speaking of Tatian in the same way, and Irenæus was his contemporary for about a half century, and Hippolytus was probably twenty years old when Tatian died.

Now, it is well known that Irenæus was the devoted pupil of Polycarp, and that Polycarp was the disciple of John, " that disciple whom Jesus loved," being more than thirty years old when John died.[1] Irenæus quotes the Gospel of John extensively, and Tatian places almost the whole of it, about ninety-six per cent—a much larger proportion than would have been possible in the case of any of the other gospels—in the *Diatessaron*. This settles the much talked of "Johannean problem," which must now retire to the shades of that limbo into which so many of the bloodless phantoms of the Tübingen School have disappeared.

An element of importance in this discussion is the answer to the question:—

---

[1] The date of Polycarp's martyrdom has been determined with a high degree of probability, as February 23d A D 155 and not in the time of Marcus Aurelius, as has long been thought, and, indeed, as Eusebius tells us. The reasons for preferring the date mentioned cannot be given here, but they are now quite generally accepted as conclusive.

V. WHEN TATIAN COMPOSED THE DIATESSARON

As to the date of the *Diatessaron*, common sense obliges us to agree with Harnack when he says, "It *cannot* have been produced during his later years, for all traces of dualism are absent."

The testimony of Irenæus is clear as to the fact that Tatian, his contemporary for about fifty years, did not teach "his peculiar form of doctrine" *till after the martyrdom of Justin.*

We find in the *Diatessaron* all those narratives and teachings which are most thoroughly out of keeping with the Encratite form of asceticism, given in full. Tatian in his latter days condemned marriage and the use of wine; but in the *Diatessaron* the account of the marriage in Cana of Galilee and the turning of water into wine is faithfully recorded, as well as Luke 7: 33, 34.

Professor Gildersleeve, in his Introduction to his edition of Justin Martyr's *Apologies*, gives preference to A.D 163 as the date of Justin's martyrdom.

The most probable time, for the composition in so laborious,[1] painstaking and reverent a

---

[1] Glancing down a page of the *Diatessaron*, we see all four of the gospels quoted in five (5) lines, so carefully are they

way, of this harmony of the four gospels, must have been *before Tatian had undergone this change*—before the simplicity of his faith had at all received the taint of that Gnosticism which was so rife in his day. The *motive* for such a work was probably strongest *when he first came to know the gospels, and when he felt the ardor of his "first love."* The most probable date, then, is soon after A. D. 150.

VI. THE DIATESSARON AS A WITNESS OF THE GOSPELS

(a) It shows that the Apocryphal Gospels, so called, are all spurious

The importance of this may not be appreciated by all; but those who have been plied with assertions that there are many other gospels as old and almost as good as four,[1] will be glad of the ability to give a ready answer; and the *Diatessaron* furnishes that answer in a most conclusive form. It contains the gospels as known to Tatian, and he a man of the widest information, born about ten years after the Apostle John died,

---

interwoven. In at least one place, all the four gospels are drawn on to make up four lines

[1] This is one of the commonest of all cavils, though, as we see, entirely baseless

knows of no gospels but those of Matthew, Mark, Luke, and John. He evidently lived before any apochryphal gospel was written, or certainly before any such writings gained any credence in the Christian Church. The very name, *Diatessaron (Διὰ Τεσσάρων)*—through four—implies that the life of our Lord was given through four gospels, and four only.

(*b*) *It absolutely overthrows the Tubingen theory as to the late origin of our four gospels.*

As we have seen, Baur dates the first three gospels from 130 to 160, and John during the decade ending A. D. 170. Since the discovery of the *Diatessaron*, honest followers of the Tubingen School have acknowledged that Baur's position was utterly untenable. Renan acknowledges that the four gospels are not spurious. Adolf Harnack, too, admits "that we learn from the *Diatessaron* that about A. D. 160, our four gospels had already taken a place of prominence in the Church, and *that no others had done so*, that in particular, the Fourth Gospel had taken a place alongside the synoptics." And, also, "that as regards the text of the gospels we can conclude from the *Diatessaron* that the text of our gospels about the year 160 already ran essentially as we now read them" (Harnack as quoted in

The Great Light from the Vatican

article on Tatian in Encyclopædia Britannica). But the *Diatessaron* proves much more than this. If we find a harmony of the four gospels prepared as early as 160, at the latest, we may conclude that these gospels had been accepted as the authoritative records of our Saviour's life, long before this time. A harmony of the gospels would not naturally come into existence immediately on the writing of the gospels. In the words of Professor Maher (*The Month*, London, November, 1892), "If Tatian, knowing the whole Church as he did, devoted himself to the construction of an elaborate harmonized gospel narrative, in which the paragraphs, texts and fragments of texts are interwoven with the utmost pains and ingenuity, and the very greatest care directed to the preservation of even the smallest words of our four gospels, it can only be because these four gospels and the least part of their contents had before this time been received by the Church, as a sacred deposit of divine truth." Now, when we think of the fact that there were then no steam printing presses, no railroads for rapid distribution, and no general councils to stamp them as authoritative, we must conclude that this result, of a general acceptance in the different districts, of all the four gospels as a divine record of Christ's life, must have required a period of many years' duration. In the words of the same writer, "The *Diatessaron* proves that, in the minds of the Christian world of that day, every sentence and syllable, every jot and tittle of these gospels possessed a peculiar sacredness. Zahn's conclusion, then, cannot be very far from the truth, 'In view of the history of the text, opinions as to the origin of John's Gospel, such as Baur has expressed, must appear simply as madness. It follows, further, that the element which remains the same in all the originals, and of the versions amid all the variations that crept into the text between A. D. 150 and 160, must have been everywhere read at the beginning of the second century.'"

They were certainly thus read as soon as the Gospel of John could be reproduced by copyists and distributed

(c) *Confirms the testimony of Irenæus and Polycarp.*

Irenæus (A. D. 200) quotes the four gospels as fully as any modern orthodox theologian would, tells us plainly that there were four gospels, and only four, and speaks of them as "Holy Scripture." Now, as we have seen,

The Great Light from the Vatican 77

Tatian was the contemporary of Irenæus for about fifty years, and Irenæus speaks of him at some length. When we consider that Tatian was the contemporary of Polycarp, the teacher of Irenæus, for more than forty years, and that Polycarp was a pupil of the Apostle John, and *his* contemporary for more than thirty years, and, then, that this Tatian prepared a harmony of the four gospels, with that of John most prominent of all, it would seem that we are warranted in saying, as we have done above, that the "Johannean problem" has vanished, and that the apostolic authority of all the gospels is established.

(*d*) *Confirms the testimony of Justin Martyr.*

The *Diatessaron* makes it certain that the "*Memoirs of the Apostles*" (ἀπομνημονεύματα τῶν ἀποστόλων, first *Apology*, 67), spoken of by Justin Martyr, as read in the worship of the Christians, were our four gospels, and not any then recent record of verbal traditions. Tatian was the pupil of Justin, and made this harmony of our four gospels, and, as we have seen, in all probability, composed his harmony in the lifetime of Justin.[1] It is not at all im-

[1] " Writers in question, more particularly, Justin, quoted, at least at times, not from our separate gospels, but from a

probable, indeed, that he did it under his supervision and with his help. Those memorials of the Saviour's life which Justin recognized as bearing the stamp of apostolic authority, and as Holy Scripture, were *our four gospels.*

The alternative would imply, to employ a quotation of Prof. Basil Gildersleeve, in commenting on these words of Justin Martyr, that "an entire change of gospels was made throughout all the different and distant provinces of the Roman Empire, at a time when concerted action through general councils was unknown, and that, too, in so silent a manner that no record of it remains in the history of the Church."

(*e*) *Confirms the testimony of the "New Syriac Gospels."*

I was at first led to believe (and, as some may know, expressed the belief) that, in these gospels, there were marks of manipulation of the account of the nativity of our Saviour in Matt. 1: 16, 21 and 25, which indicated that

---

harmony of the gospels."—(*Rendel Harris' Diatessaron of Tatian,* p 54)

We know that Tatian wrote such a harmony. That was not published till after Justin's death , but it would not be improbable that some sort of rough draft might have been used by both master and scholar before its publication."— *Dr W Sanday, Bampton Lectures,* p 301

this Syriac text was used in the propagation of the Cerinthian heresy; and Cerinthus was a younger contemporary of the Apostle John (See Prof. J. Rendell Harris's Art. in *Contemporary Review*, November, 1894). This, if true, would seem to show that the four gospels were not only written, but already gathered together, recognized, by heretics as well as the orthodox, as the authoritative records of Christianity, and then translated into Syriac; and that, in the lifetime of a contemporary of the Apostle John. The *Diatessaron* adds much to the probability that Professor Harris's conclusion is true, so far as the age of these Syriac gospels is concerned. It shows marks of the Curetonian Syriac text, and, according to Prof. Harris, this is a revised version of the "New Syriac Gospels" in the interest of orthodoxy. It would seem, then, that these *Lewis gospels, or Sinaitic palimpsest*, were, so to speak, two generations earlier than the *Diatessaron*, and that they must have been translated near the beginning of the second century.

Mrs. Lewis, the discoverer of the *Sinaitic palimpsest*, dissents from Dr. Harris's opinion that the version was Cerinthian in character, saying that "some of the most eminent scholars in England, France, and Germany, including Dr. Westcott, have pronounced in favor of its orthodoxy."

However this point may be decided, there is little if any doubt of the very early origin of this translation of the four gospels. The *Diatessaron* is good evidence on this point. Whether the *Sinaitic* or the *Curetonian* is the earlier Syriac version, may be left to the critics to discuss, and if they can do so, decide; but that both are older than the *Diatessaron* there can be little doubt, as peculiar readings of both these versions are found in it.

The *Diatessaron*, then, shows that both these versions must have been made early in the second century; and *one* of them *may* have been made before it began.

The only alternative, evidently, is that a Syriac version, the ancestor, so to speak, of both of these, was that from which the *Diatessaron* was composed, and for the settling of the main question, the genuineness of the gospels, this would amount to the same thing. It is well nigh certain that both these versions precede the *Diatessaron*, and it has been generally thought that another Syriac version preceded *them*.

The *Diatessaron* and *Sinaitic palimpsest* both

The Great Light from the Vatican 81

lack the account of the woman taken in adultery. This is a characteristic of the earliest texts. But the *Sinaitic* also lacks the last chapter of Mark after the eighth verse, while the *Diatessaron* has it. This is one of the many signs that the *Sinaitic* is earlier than the *Diatessaron*. It also shows that the *Diatessaron* drew on some source other than the *Siniatic* (the Curetonian ?), for this part of its text.

CONCLUSION

VII. THE DIATESSARON, AN INDEPENDENT WITNESS

When the *Diatessaron* is spoken of as confirming the testimony of so many other witnesses, it should not be inferred that its testimony is in any sense *dependent* on theirs While it makes clearer and more conclusive the testimony which each of them gives, its own would stand unimpeachable, even on the impossible supposition that theirs could be refuted. Among all these witnesses it occupies a unique position. It is the only copy of the gospels of that early time *that is known to have come from the pen of a well-known historical character*. It is as certain that Tatian prepared this harmony from the four gospels in a complete form as any fact of that date can be to us. This, of course, absolutely fixes its date within the narrow limits of a very few years of Tatian's life. Other versions were certainly earlier, at least the one from which this harmony was composed; but the age of each one has to be determined by internal marks. The age of *this* is settled *historically* and without reference to those internal signs by which specialists determine the date of texts.

Pharos, the world's wonder, reared its marble shaft far aloft, and threw its great light over all the approaches to Alexandria, showing the positions of other landmarks doubtless; but without reference to them, *its* position was well known to all the world, and if *they* had been swept away, *it* would still have served its own great purpose.

Thus, we see the *Diatessaron*—the fourfold gospel—standing about a half century after John as a monumental witness of the genuineness of the gospels which furnish those facts that are the foundation of our faith—facts concerning God's merciful intervention to save the lost through Jesus Christ, whom he hath anointed and named Jesus because "he shall save his people from their sins"—and revealing to us, so to speak, the locations of other

The Great Light from the Vatican 83

beacons still nearer the shore and shining with the light of all the gospels.

In plain words, while its own testimony is clear and indubitable, it also serves to emphasize and confirm that of the contemporaries of Tatian, Irenæus, Justin, and Polycarp, and shows us that, in the Syriac version or versions from which it was composed, the Syrian Christians had their need supplied by copies of the four gospels, complete and distinct, made still earlier.

We may appeal to the common sense of all honest men, and ask, in view of all these facts:

Is it credible that if the gospels had been forgeries, the great company of Syrian Christians would have received, as a part of the Holy Scriptures, these versions made, when there were still living thousands of Christians who were contemporaries of the Apostle John in their youth? The improbability is too great to be entertained for a moment.

The only rational conclusion is that the gospels thus early received as authoritative, translated, and combined into a harmony, *were* so received and prepared for use because they are genuine—written by the persons whose names they have borne from the first; and that they had the stamp of apostolic approval.

IV.

THE FULLER LIGHT FROM MOUNT SINAI

At Cambridge, England, there live two ladies who may well be numbered among the heroines of our times. Distinguished as scholars at one of the world's chief centers of learning, instrumental in securing, by their munificence, the establishment there of the youngest of its sisterhood of colleges, and surrounded by all that could contribute to social enjoyment and the pleasures of learned ease, they have yet endured hardships and faced dangers from which most *men* would shrink, to accomplish a great work for the benefit of our own and succeeding generations.

In recent years many discoveries have been made which serve to throw welcome light on that most interesting of all books, the Bible; but few of these surpass in interest and importance those made by the twin sisters, Mrs. Lewis and Mrs. Gibson of Cambridge, in February, 1892. Of these discoveries the most important was that of a Syriac manuscript

The Fuller Light from Mount Sinai 85

containing the four gospels; a manuscript more than fourteen centuries old, a copy of a Syriac version made, as very eminent scholars think, not many years after the death of the Apostle John. The manuscript was complete with the exception of a few of the vellum leaves which had been lost.

It is interesting to notice the train of events which led these ladies to make their journey to Mount Sinai.

Prof. Rendel Harris had made the discovery of the long-lost *Apology of Aristides* in the library of this convent in 1889. He was led to make his researches in that place by the fact that the indefatigable efforts of Tischendorf had resulted in the discovery there, in 1859, of the Sinaitic Codex, which is considered by many scholars the very oldest copy of the Bible in existence, not excepting even the Vatican Codex, at Rome.

Tischendorf had seen some leaves of this celebrated manuscript in a wastebasket in the convent in 1844; and now, under the authority of the Czar of Russia, he had come again to make an exhaustive search for the remainder of the Codex of which he saw that they formed a part. After several weeks of fruitless effort he was about to depart. He had ordered his Bedawin to have his dromedaries ready for the return journey; when, taking a walk in the evening with the steward of the convent among the surpassingly interesting scenes of Sinai, he was invited, on returning, to take tea in the latter's cell. He had been speaking, probably, of his disappointment in not finding the remainder of the copy of the Septuagint, a fragment of which he had seen in the wastebasket fifteen years before, when the steward casually remarked that he too had been interested in reading the Septuagint lately, and, going to a corner of the cell brought back a bulkly volume wrapped in a red cloth, and laid it in Tischendorf's hands. The scholar, after the first glance, was assured that he had before him the long-sought treasure. Here were the leaves matching those he had seen on his former visit, and containing a large part of the rest of the Old Testament, together with the New, to which were appended the *Epistle of Barnabas* and the *Shepherd of Hermas*.

But, Prof. Rendel Harris was not the only one whose zeal for discovery was awakened and stimulated by Tischendorf's success Mrs. Lewis tells us that in early girlhood, the desire came upon her to visit this old convent, founded by Justinian at Mount Sinai, and that when many years afterwards, the way was opened for her to go, it was with something like assurance that some important discovery would be the result.

Mrs. Lewis and her sister, Mrs. Gibson, seem, providentially, to have received a training, from childhood on, by which they were fitted to do their remarkable work for the world. The children of a wealthy Scotch gentleman, their education was very carefully conducted by competent instructors under the direction and supervision of their father. They, probably, early exhibited a love for languages, with a facility in acquiring a knowledge of them; and, to encourage them in these pursuits, as soon as they learned a language well, they were allowed, as a reward, to make a journey, and spend some time among the people who spoke it. Thus it came about, doubtless, that in later years they could converse with equal ease, with ecclesiastics who spoke modern Greek, and Bedawin, whose talk, during their many camel journeys through the desert, was in Arabic.

But the account of the journey to Mount Sinai, along the track of the Exodus of Israel, would better be told in Mrs. Lewis's own words:

"The project of visiting Sinai came first into my mind in early girlhood, when my future brother-in-law, Mr. James Young Gibson, traveled by Sinai and Petra to Jerusalem in 1865, and his glowing descriptions of desert scenery were forever haunting my memory It was revived after a very successful journey, which my sister and I made through Greece in 1883. The hospitality which we had received from Greek monks, and the pleasant intercourse which we had enjoyed with Greek ecclesiastics, emboldened us to think that a visit to the Sinai Convent would be profitable, and that perhaps our knowledge of Arabic might facilitate our intercourse with the Bedawin who would escort us thither. I made an attempt to carry out this design in 1886, but I got no farther than 'Uyun Musa, being deterred by apprehensions about the health of a lady friend who was traveling with me.'

"After my marriage in 1887 to the Rev. Samuel Savage Lewis, of Corpus Christi College, Cambridge, we made several Oriental journeys together; but I had to relinquish all thoughts of Sinai, as my husband was bound to residence in his college during February, the only season of the year when a desert journey is compatible with health."

Mr. Lewis died suddenly in 1891, and Mr. James Y. Gibson, the husband of her sister had died also. In the summer of this year the Syriac text of Professor Harris's then new discovery, the *Apology of Aristides*, was published. Mrs. Lewis became much interested in this defense of the early Christians, which, Eusebius informs us, the Greek philosopher, Aristides, who had become a Christian, presented to the Emperor, Hadrian, when he came to Athens to be initiated in the Eleusinian Mysteries in the eighth year of his reign, *i. e.*, in 124 or 125 of our era. She gave herself to earnest study of the Syriac, especially in the ancient Estrangelo character, which her knowledge of Hebrew and Arabic, both languages of the same family, made quite easy. Rev. R. H. Kennett of Queen's College was her instructor.

Meeting with the wife of Professor Harris with whom she had been very slightly acquainted before this, she told her that she was busily engaged in the study of the *Apology* in the Syriac, and that she intended to go to Mount Sinai. Dr. Harris immediately called and taught the sisters to photograph with his own camera to prepare them for their work there, and, to use Mrs. Lewis's words, "expressed the opinion so decidedly that there were treasures in the convent which he had not thoroughly examined, that we both looked forward to our journey with the brightest expectations. For several weeks I dreamed of the dark closet so vividly described to me by Dr. Harris, in which lay the two mysterious chests full of manuscripts, and to which access was only to be obtained by propitiating the reverend recluses who owned them. So strongly were we impressed with the idea that we were going to discover something, that the night before our departure when the Master of Corpus (Dr. Perowne) and Mr. Kennett both called to say farewell, they actually speculated on what the discovery was to be; and Mr. Kennett expressed a hope that it might be the *Harmony of the Four Gospels* (or Diatessaron) written by Tatian in the second century." [The epoch-making discovery of this remarkable work in an Arabic translation had been made in the Vatican Library a few years before this. The hope was that the original Syriac might be found.] Several Oriental scholars were invited to accompany Mrs. Lewis and her sister, Mrs. Gibson to Mount Sinai, but all efforts in this direction having failed, the two sisters braved the journey without them.

The Fuller Light from Mount Sinai

Dr. Rendel Harris, however, though unable to go with them at this time, did much to prepare for and further their success. Says Mrs. Lewis: "Dr. Harris very kindly ordered a half-plate camera for us with all its appurtenances, and also designed a manuscript stand for our use to obviate some of the difficulties which he had experienced."

The journey was by way of Cairo, and an introduction to the patriarch of Alexandria secured one from him, or rather, from his representative (he himself being absent), to the Archbishop of Mount Sinai, who received them most kindly. This insured their favorable reception at the St. Catherine Convent on Mount Sinai; which is thus described, after mention of incidents of the journey:—

"Next day we climbed the pass of Nug Hawa on foot, followed by our dromedaries. Soon the peak of Ras Sufsafeh burst on our view, and we stood on the great plain of Er-Rahah, just before the mountain which burned with fire, where the voice of God was heard in thunder by the multitude beneath. At length, the convent appeared in view, nestling in a narrow valley, surrounded by a walled garden, and overlooked on the one hand by the cliffs of Jebel Mousa, and on the other, by a mountain named after two Greek saints, Galakteon and Episteme.

"While our tents were being pitched beside a well of delicious water, amid the cypresses, olives, and flowering almond trees of the garden, we were received by the Hegoumenos, or prior, and by Galakteon, the librarian, whose eyes sparkled with sincere pleasure when he read our letter to himself from Mr. Rendel Harris, 'The world is not so large after all,' he exclaimed, 'when we can have real friends in such distant lands.'"

This aged and amiable librarian gave them not only the fullest liberty to examine the treasures of which he was the custodian, but all possible personal assistance. "On Monday, February 8th," Mrs. Lewis continues, "we worked for seven hours in the library, beginning at 9 A. M. The manuscripts were very much scattered, some Greek ones being in the show library, and the Arabic partly there, and partly in a little room halfway up a dark stair.

"The Syriac ones, and those supposed to be the most ancient, are partly in this room, and partly in a dark closet approached through a room almost as dark. There they repose in two closed boxes, and cannot be seen without a lighted candle. They have, at different times, been stored in vaults beneath the convent for safety, when attacks were threatened by the Bedawin.

"They were there exposed to damp and then allowed to dry without any care. It is a wonder that the strong parchment and clearly written letters have, in so many cases, withstood so many adverse influences.

"Galakteon gave us every facility for photographing. He spent hours holding books open for us, or deciphering pages of the Septuagint. The fact that the English should be so anxious for a correct version of the sacred writings as to have sheets of paper printed on purpose for scholars to collate them with all the extant manuscripts, filled the monks with a profound respect. The only drawback to our comfort was the bitterly cold wind. As there was no glass in the library windows, we had some difficulty in keeping ourselves warm. This we could only do by a smart walk out of the narrow wady."

It was among these ill-kept manuscripts on vellum that the one now known as *The Sinaitic* or *Lewis palimpsest*, was found. As we shall see farther on, Mrs. Lewis thinks, that owing to a more recent discovery connected with its history, it should be renamed, *The Antiochene palimpsest.*

She tells us, "I had never before seen a palimpsest, but my father had often related to us wonderful stories of how the old monks, when vellum had become scarce and paper was not yet invented, scraped away the writing from the pages of their books and wrote something new on the top of it; and how after the lapse of ages, the old ink was revived by the action of the common air, and the old words peeped up again; and how a text of Plato had come to light in this curious way."

Among other manuscripts they found one of 538 pages, a palimpsest, written in Syriac. Many of its leaves were glued together, and some had to be separated by the woman-like expedient of holding them over the steam of a teakettle. The eyes of these sisters were probably the first that had looked on these old characters, one set of them almost hidden behind another, for many centuries. Says Mrs. Lewis:—

"I saw at once that this manuscript contained two writings, both in the same ancient Estrangelo character, which I had been studying; that the upper writing was the biographies of women saints, and bore its own date, which I read, 1,009 years after Alexander, A. D. 697; and that the underwriting was the gospels. The latter was written in two columns, one of which always projected onto the margin of the upper writing, so that many of its words could be easily read, and every word distinctly belonged to the sacred narrative. I pointed this out to my sister, and, as if to make assurance doubly sure, I showed her also that at the top of almost every page stood the title 'Evangelium, of Matthew, of Mark,' or 'of Luke.' I felt sure that this text of the gospels must be at least 200 years older than the one which superseded (or sat upon) it, and could not therefore be later than the fifth century. . . .

"My reasons for placing a high value on the palimpsest were noted down in my journal, under date of February 11th, and were afterwards embodied in an account of our journey which was printed for *The Presbyterian Churchman* of June, July, and August, before we had asked any of our friends to examine the gospel text."

It is amusing to learn from Mrs. Lewis's account, of how trivial a possibility was dreaded which might destroy all the fruits of their photographic labors. That dread was that the customs officials might mistake the rolled films containing their photographs for rolls of tobacco and should let in the light and destroy them. This, happily, did not occur.

Though Mrs. Lewis understood that the discovery was one of great importance, it was many months before even she came to understand how very important it was, and what a place it was soon to take among the irrefragable testimonies to the genuineness of the four gospels. A severe illness which Mrs. Gibson suffered after the return of the sisters to their home in Cambridge delayed the critical examination of the manuscript for a considerable time. On July 15th of the year of the discovery, 1892, they invited a company of friends to luncheon and, before the departure of Mr. and Mrs. F. C. Burkitt, who were among them, brought some of the photographs and spread them on the piano for the inspection of the young Syriac scholar. Mrs. Lewis told him that the underwriting was Syriac Gospels, and hoped that he might be able " with his keen young eyes" to decipher them. He became deeply interested and asked her permission to take about a dozen of the photographs home with him for careful examination. She readily assented to this request, and, on the second day after this, received from Mrs. Burkitt the following note:—

"12 *Harvey Road*

"MY DEAR MRS. LEWIS —Frank is in a state of the highest excitement He wrote down a part of the palimpsest last night, and has been in to Dr. Bensley's with it, and they have discovered it is a part of the Cureton Syriac. Do you know, only one copy exists! You can imagine Frank's glee! He has just been in to tell me, and run back to the Bensleys'. I thought you would be interested and write at once   I am yours affectionately,
A. PERSIS BURKITT."

On the day after the receipt of the note a meeting of those most interested in the discovery was held at the house of Professor Bensley, and as it was clear that the manuscript could not be fully and accurately copied except from the original at Mount Sinai, a second expedition was decided on for the accomplishment of that purpose. Prof. Rendel Harris was invited by the sisters to accompany them, together with Professor Bensley and Mr. F. C. Burkitt and their wives. The party rendezvoused at Suez on June 27th and proceeded to their destination, the convent of St. Catherine, where they were most cordially received by the monks.

"The next morning," says Mrs. Lewis, "Galakteon tottered into what was called the archbishop's room, where the Syriac books were kept, and asked what we wished to see first." The reply, of course was, "all the books photographed last year." *The Palestinian Lectionary* which has since been edited and published by Mrs. Lewis in a very elaborate and elegant form, was intrusted to her that she might work on it in her tent, and the palimpsest was divided between the three gentlemen for decipherment and transcription so far as this very difficult task might prove possible.

While the discovery of the palimpsest has given Mrs. Lewis celebrity among scholars the world over, her edition of the Lectionary, has obtained for her the honorary degree of Doctor of Philosophy from the united faculty of Halle-Wittenberg, and the name of her sister, Mrs. Gibson, was honorably mentioned in her diploma.

Many readers may not be able to understand why Mr. Burkitt should have been excited by his supposed discovery that the palimpsest was a copy of the Cureton Syriac manuscript of the gospels. It was not simply because there was but one copy of this fragmentary manuscript of the gospels which was brought by Archdeacon Tattam from the Nitrian desert and deposited with others which he brought with it in the British Museum in 1842, but because Canon Cureton who discovered its characteristics and published it in 1858, had come to the conclusion that it was the oldest manuscript of the gospels in Syriac discovered up to that time. The fact that it was fragmentary would make the discovery of a second copy of greater importance from the fact that passages missing in the first copy might be supplied from the second. The Cureton manuscript had, for instance, only a few verses of the Gospel of Mark, and another copy might contain all of that gospel.

The scholars had not worked long at their task when they found that though the text before them had points of likeness to that of the Cureton manuscript, it was not a second copy of the same. Mrs. Lewis says: "It was of the same character, but more concise, and apparently more ancient by half a century."

She also says: "Mr. Harris pronounced it to be by no means a difficult palimpsest, but the pages varied greatly in distinctness, and though even I could trace the words, being of their natural size, as I could not do in my photographs, there were many from which the ink of the underwriting had faded leaving only faint indications on the vellum from which words could be traced. Add to this that many of these words were covered by the dark upperwriting which was, happily, of a different color, and that most of it had to be read between the lines, and my readers may appreciate the difficulty of the task which was to be undertaken."

Before going to Mount Sinai the second time Mrs. Lewis procured four bottles of a chemical compound which was of great use in this difficult work of deciphering the manuscripts. She did not at first use it. "For ten days," says she, "I had to restrain my impatience about using this; but on the eleventh, I happened to open a large volume of Mar Isaac's discourses, which I had known on our former visit, and which contained many passages so faded as to be quite illegible. I asked Galakteon to let me restore one of these, with the result that it came up of a brilliant hue of dark green, and he was so astonished that he asked me to paint up the whole volume and then to try my 'scent-bottle,' as it was called, on other hoary documents.

"How triumphant I felt when he gave me permission to touch up the palimpsest, though only in a few places where it could not be read otherwise! Professor Bensley at first disapproved of the proceeding, but as both his fellow-workers gave my brush the warmest welcome, he was induced, after a few days to ask for it himself, and many a blank margin thus became covered with very distinct writing."

Forty days of hard work were spent by the indefatigable scholars in research among the treasures of the convent, in deciphering and transcribing. But though very laborious days, they must have been very happy ones. The joy of discovery, the gratification of finding, day by day, increasing proof of the inestimable value of the chief treasure which had been brought to light, the reflex energies normally employed,—in this case, the highest energies of noble minds,—the daily intercourse in work and rest, and above all, the wonderful surroundings; scenes of the exquisite beauty of subtropical foliage, set off by the grandeur of those bare rocky heights, sublime, solitary, awe-inspiring, from which God once vouchsafed the most august revelation which the human race has ever received, must have filled those days of strenuous toil with a unique interest and inspiration. The time must have been happily spent as it passed and will, doubtless, be a bright spot in the memories of those who had the privilege of taking part in this great work. Yet, as is often the case in our experience, the memories of this happy period will always be chastened by the recollection of sorrow. Professor Bensley fell sick in Rome, on the return journey, and died three days after reaching his home at Cambridge, and, a few weeks later, the old librarian Galakteon, who had done so much to forward the plans of his European friends, was gathered to his fathers, "as a shock of corn cometh in in his season."

After all the learned labor expended by the distinguished scholars at Mount Sinai, many passages were left undeciphered, and others were subjects of conjecture rather than of certain knowledge. This being the case, Mrs. Lewis and Mrs. Gibson made a third journey to the scene of the discovery in January, 1895.

The Archbishop of Mount Sinai, Porphyrios, offered them every facility for investigating, but when they asked for the palimpsest, the new librarian after a vain search, informed them that it was not to be found in the library. This was surprising, because Mrs Lewis had provided a handsome box for the manuscript that it might be preserved from injury in the future, and Mrs. Bensley had prepared a silk cover for it with the same design. It was known to the sisters that some pages of other manuscripts had been stolen from the convent, and it now looked as if the palimpsest of the gospels might have met a similar fate. We can well believe that, as Mrs. Lewis says, they had "a bad quarter of an hour." But in the midst of their dismay, Euthumios, the successor of Galakteon, was seen approaching with the manuscript enveloped in its silk cover, and their anxiety was immediately turned into joy. During this visit, and another which the sisters made to the convent in 1897, the palimpsest was examined with the greatest care, and many of the gaps in the first transcription were filled. Many of the former readings were satisfactorily verified, while in some cases, corrections were made.

A NEW DISCOVERY

By the almost incredible labor which had now been bestowed on this most interesting copy of the gospels, it would seem that it must have been made to yield all its secrets to the learned investigators. Strange as it may seem, however, all these examinations of the original manuscript failed to bring to light an important fact in the history of the palimpsest which has been made known by the photographs of its last two pages. This fact is that it was not made a palimpsest at Sinai, but at Antioch, where "the disciples were first called Christians."[1]

For a full description of the palimpsest and its peculiar features we may go to the series of articles now passing through *The Expository Times* on "What have we gained in the Sinaitic Palimpsest." The palimpsest itself is, also, accessible to the English readers in a translation made by the discoverer.[2]

As to the palimpsest's testimony for the gospels, it is only necessary to mention a few facts, to see

One of these is that it contains our four gospels, and no others, indicating that the so-called *Apocryphal Gospels*, were unknown, or at least, unacknowledged as having any authority, when this translation was made.

---

[1] For an account of this remarkable discovery as to the place where the four gospels were turned into a palimpsest by writing over them the lives of women saints by 'John, the Recluse," see the article, *The earlier Home of the Sinaitic Palimpsest*, in *The Expositor* for June, 1900

[2] For a fuller account of the discovery of the palimpsest and of the journey to Mount Sinai the reader is referred to Mrs Gibson's "How the Codex was Found," and Mrs Lewis's, "In the Shadow of Sinai."

Another is, that it must have been made very early. The *Diatessaron*, a harmony of the four gospels, prepared by Tatian, probably in the decade 150–160 is found to contain a number of readings, or turns of expression, found only in this *Sinaitic Palimpsest*, indicating that this version (or else one from which it was, in part, copied), must have been in existence before the *Diatessaron*

This version is a translation of the *whole of the four gospels*, and the text has marked characteristics of the earliest Greek manuscripts: "a text," as Professor Harris, in his able article in *The Contemporary*, November, 1894, remarks, " that often agrees with all that is most ancient in Greek manuscripts, a text which the advanced critic will at once acknowledge to be, after allowance has been made for a few serious blemishes, superior in quality to all extant copies, with a very few exceptions." These "serious blemishes," as he considers them, are all found in three verses of the first chapter of Matthew.

This shows that the theory of the *gradual evolution* of the gospels is a dream.

Another fact to be considered is that this is a *translation*, implying an original from which it was translated, existing therefore still earlier than this version which Professor Harris concludes "must have been made far back in the second century."

It is interesting in this connection, to notice that Prof. Adolf Harnack of Berlin, though viewing the question from his far-from-orthodox standpoint, has at last acknowledged the force of the accumulating evidence that all the gospels were written within the first century. Recent discoveries have forced him to this conclusion; and, after mentioning the *Apology of Aristides* and *The Diatessaron of Tatian*, he says:—

"But of still greater value was the find which we owe to a learned Scotch lady, Mrs. Lewis. . . .

"As the text is almost completely preserved this *Syrus Sinaiticus* is one of the most important witnesses; nay it is extremely probable that it is the most important witness, for our gospels" (see his article in *Preussische Jahrbucher*, May, 1898).

Standing, like Harnack, in the van of German scholarship, Prof. Theodor Zahn of Erlangen has given his conclusions as to the dates of the gospels, respectively, as follows:—

Matthew, in Aramaic, 62; in Greek, 85;

Mark (prepared) 64; Mark (published) 67; Luke 75; John 80-90. Harnack's dates are Mark, 65-70; Matthew, 70-75; Luke 78-90; John, "not later than the beginning of the second century."[1]

Thus, the two most noted New Testament scholars in Germany, the leaders of the two opposing scholars of criticism, have by independent researches from different standpoints, been brought to almost identical conclusions as to the dates of the gospels; dates not inconsistent with the authorship of contemporaries of Christ. Harnack, brought, or, I may say, forced, to this conclusion by the external evidence of recent discoveries, finds it confirmed by the internal evidence of the documents themselves, and says:—

"In their essential substance, the gospels belong to the first, the Jewish, aspect of Christianity, that brief epoch which may be denoted as the palæontological."

The views of such critics as Abbott and Schmiedel published in the Encyclopædia Bib-

---

[1] Blass thinks that Luke wrote his gospel during the imprisonment of Paul at Cæsarea A D 54-56, according to his reckoning, 57-59 according to that of Ramsay See *The Homiletic Review*, December, 1900 "Pauline Chronology," by W M Ramsay, and *The Churchman* (London) "The Western Text of St Luke" by W Harloe Dundas.

lica are due to vision distorted and judgment warped by the prepossessions of their own minds. Of the attack of these critics and others like them, Canon Gore (now Bishop of Worcester), himself a higher critic, well remarks: "Now, it is easy to magnify the importance of the movement, and even to overestimate its men. It has no discovery in early Christian literature to start from. The great discoveries of those years have all gone toward the confirmation of the traditional faith." . . .

"They are discovered constantly asserting that things 'cannot have been as they are represented in the gospels,' either because they do not square with the writer's own conception of Jesus and his times, or because they contradict some of his philosophical ideas, such as the impossibility of miracle."

Even Wendt has announced his conclusion that, "critical inquiry has led, though not immediately in its first attempts, yet gradually in the course of time, to results whereby the historical picture of Jesus has lost nothing, but only gained."

And David Smith of Tulliallan, who quotes this saying of Wendt, gives this statement of the results of that New Testament criticism by which so many have been alarmed and some have been robbed of their faith :—

"The history of New Testament criticism is the record of the rise and fall of a thousand theories, each influential and seemingly final, for a brief space, and each abandoned in its turn; and the New Testament has outlived them all, as it will outlive their successors to the end of time. $E\xi\eta\rho\acute{a}\nu\vartheta\eta$ $\acute{o}$ $\chi\acute{o}\rho\tau o\varsigma$," etc

Yes, truly, "The grass withereth, and the flower thereof falleth away: but the word of the Lord endureth forever."

These words forcibly emphasize the famous reply of Beza to Henry of Navarre: "It is true, sire, that it is the part of the Church of God to receive blows and return none; but, remember that it is *an anvil* that has used up many hammers" (a usé beaucoup de marteaux).

The blows of the hammers are falling still, but the "anvil" is as firmly fixed as ever, and we may be sure that in God's good providence the criticism of the Scriptures now so prevalent will be overruled for the furtherance of the gospel in the end Criticism may develop, for one thing, into a sane Biblical Theology, which will lead to the deeper and more enthusiastic study of the Bible, and the most searching investigations will tend to establish confidence in it, though in some persons, that confidence may for the time, be weakened or destroyed.

"Truth's like a torch: the more it's shook it shines," and we may believe with well grounded assurance that the revelation God has given will give forth its light more clearly through the discussion of it, and that the hand of criticism, which some feared would extinguish it, grown more wisely skillful, will but make it shine more brightly; yea, will put it on a pinnacle to send forth more clearly its beacon light for the salvation of a lost world.

V.

TWIN LIGHTS FROM ATHENS

I. ARISTIDES AND QUADRATUS, THE COMPANION APOLOGISTS

JUSTIN MARTYR had stood in the Church's view, for ages, at the head of the brave band of defenders of the faith, the apologists of the second century; but the discovery of the *Apology of Aristides* in the St. Catherine Convent in 1889 has given to its author the first place. Aristides now takes precedence.

But another, perhaps still more eminent Christian, Quadratus, presented a defense of the Christians at the same time with Aristides

Of this event Eusebius gives the following account :—

"But Trajan," [who became emperor of Rome before the death of the Apostle John], "having held the sovereignty twenty years wanting six months, is succeeded in the imperial office by Ælius Hadrian. To him Quadratus addressed a discourse as an apology for the religion which we profess, because certain malicious persons attempted to harass the brethren.

"The work is *still in the hands of some of the brethren, as also in our own*, from which any one may see evident proof of the understanding of the man and of his *apostolic* faith." [Italics mine.] Indicating the early date at which Quadratus began his work, Eusebius continues: "This writer shows the antiquity of the age in which he lived, in these passages:

"'The deeds of our Saviour,' says he, 'were always before you, for they were true miracles; those that were healed, those that were raised from the dead, who were seen, not only when healed and when raised, but were always present. They remained living a long time, not only whilst our Lord was on earth, but likewise when he had left the earth, so that *some of them have also lived to our own times*.' Such was Quadratus." Eusebius continues:—

"Aristides, also, a man faithfully devoted to the religion we profess, like Quadratus, has left to posterity a defense of the faith addressed to Adrian. This work is, also, preserved by a great number, even to the present day."

Thus, twenty-five years after the death of the Apostle John, there occurred this event of thrilling interest. At Athens, and, possibly,

Twin Lights from Athens

on that very Mars' Hill where Paul preached, and where the court of the Areopagus held its sessions, or it may be, on the adjacent summit of the Acropolis, crowned with that paragon of architecture, the Parthenon, with its frieze of Phidias, its inimitable ivory and gold Athena, within, and its colossal Athena, without, these two brave men, Aristides, the Athenian philosopher, who had become a Christian, and Quadratus, the evangelist,—the first, possibly a young man filled with enthusiasm at finding in the gospel a philosophy infinitely transcending the noblest product even of the Greek intellect—the other almost certainly an old man, with a life of loving labors chiefly behind him, came to acknowledge in the most public way their allegiance to their Lord. This they did by presenting to Hadrian, the Emperor of Rome, a plea for their persecuted brethren and their much-misrepresented faith.

The brave deed was not destined to be fruitless. Not only was the " Rescript of Hadrian " by which the severity of the persecution was greatly mitigated, in all probability, a result of it, but it must have served to cheer and strengthen the persecuted Christian host that stood trembling behind them, its leaders, by its high example of Christian heroism.

114   *New Light on the New Testament*

The martyrologies of the middle ages, even, presented the tradition of the brave and brilliant deed, and now the *Apology of Aristides* has come forth from its concealment of many centuries as one of the witnesses to encourage faith, in an age of doubt.

Eusebius tells us that the *Apology of Quadratus* " was in his hands and in those of some of the brethren."[1] He gives us a specimen which makes us long to see the whole of it. The extract from it which we have indicates how early he had lived. Irenæus tells of Polycarp at whose feet he had sat in his youth, and Quadratus could probably tell of John and possibly, even of Paul and Peter, as he was of those who, in the words of Eusebius, "held the first rank in the apostolic succession," and who had seen those who were the subjects of our Saviour's miracles.

What a chasm this *Apology of Quadratus* if recovered, would bridge! The half century from A. D. 75 to 125 is almost a blank to us. We have scarcely any particulars about it, and yet, in these fifty years there took place the

---

[1] "The *Apology of Quadratus* seems to have survived till the 6th century for several passages are quoted in the controversy between the monk Andrew and Eusebius (86), Photius, Cod. 162 "—Dr George Salmon in *Dict. of Xn Biography*.

greatest movement of all church history since the days of the apostles. The letter of a heathen, written about twelve years after John's body was laid to rest at Ephesus, throws an interesting sidelight on it. Trajan's governor of Bithynia, Pliny, writing to his master, speaks of the heathen temples "almost deserted," of "great numbers involved in the dangers of these persecutions," which were then in progress, while he asserts that "this contagious superstition is not confined to the cities only, but has spread its infection among the country villages." He tells Trajan of "this inquiry having already extended, and being still likely to extend to persons of all ages and ranks, and of both sexes" Such is the view of the results of this period of evangelization which a Roman governor has from the outside of the Christian community, and with eyes hostile to it. It is the view of a contemporary and one who is a very competent witness as far as intelligence is concerned.

Eusebius gives, at a much later time, the inside view of the agencies—the human agencies at least—which brought about these wonderful results. But he had before him the words of earlier writers who were not only witnesses within the Christian circle, but agents in the glorious work. Eusebius knew of others, but he makes a more honorable mention of none than of Quadratus. He says:—

"Of those who flourished in these times, Quadratus is said to have been distinguished for prophetical gifts. There were many others, also noted in these times, who held the first rank in the apostolic succession. These, as the holy disciples of such men, also built up the churches where foundations had been laid in every place by the apostles. They augmented the means of promulgating the gospel more and more, and spread the seeds of salvation and of the heavenly kingdom throughout the world, far and wide. For the most of the disciples at that time, animated with a more ardent love of the divine word, had first fulfilled the Saviour's precept by distributing their substance to the needy. Afterwards, leaving their country, they performed the office of evangelists to those who had not yet heard the faith; whilst with a noble ambition, they delivered to them the books of the holy gospel. After laying the foundation of the gospel in foreign parts, as the particular object of their mission, and after appointing others as shepherds of the flocks, and committing to these the care of those that had been recently introduced, they went again to other regions and nations, with the grace and coöperation of God. The Holy Spirit also wrought many wonders, as yet, through them, so that as soon as the gospel was heard, men voluntarily, and in crowds, eagerly embraced the true faith with their whole minds."

Oh, glorious, golden age of Christianity, prophecy and promise, we trust, of a still more glorious golden age to come, when, after these times of worldliness and dearth, God will pour out his spirit upon all flesh! Quadratus had been, perhaps, for fifty years among these scenes so blessed and yet so full at times of suffering. Now is a time of suffering, and the old hero comes with his defense, and along with the philosopher Aristides, appeals to the emperor in behalf of the Christians. God seems to have blessed the brave deed. The "Rescript of Hadrian" to Fundanus, the proconsul of Asia, was issued after it, commanding that no Christian should be punished without examination and proof.

Now, what a boon would the full account of this glorious and yet terrible half century, written by a contemporary and thoroughly competent witness, be! For one reason one would like to live fifty years more. It is to be hoped that within that time the long lost *Apology of Quadratus* will be discovered, as that of Aristides has been already. Eusebius had it before him when he wrote his history, and gives us a very appetizing and very tantalizing morsel. What a flood of light would the rediscovered *Apology* shed on this glorious and yet almost wholly unknown half century!

Before this period we have the simplicity of apostolic Christianity. Soon after it we find the beginnings, at least of that intricate and artificial ecclesiasticism, which so sadly transformed and deformed the pure religion of Christ. The multiform errors of Gnosticism, that "hydra-headed monster," as Hippolytus calls it, that with the many forms of heathen philosophies and religions, served to adulterate and ruin so much of the nominal Christianity of the time, soon came upon the scene. The influences which wrought the sad change were working, doubtless, in secret, through all this long period, but we cannot trace them. All is dim and indistinct, and to some extent uncertain, through all this tract of time. We know something of some characters in it, but they are to us at this distance like men seen through a mist, across wide gorges among mountain heights—magnified, shadowy forms, standing, we cannot tell just where, and moving, we scarcely know whither.

What a boon a flood of clear light on this period would be! That light the *Apology of Quadratus*, if discovered, will probably give in such a way as no other known writing does. He was a man qualified to tell of these times intelligently and reliably; and from the quotations of Eusebius from his *Apology* and from what Eusebius says of him, we see that he must have told much that would be intensely interesting to us after almost eighteen centuries.

II. THE APOLOGY OF ARISTIDES DISCOVERED

Let us now turn to the *Apology* which Aristides addressed to Hadrian.

We can only indulge hopes of the discovery of the *Apology of Quadratus;* that of his companion apologist is now in our hands, coming to us in two languages, and in two different forms, in one of which we have it in its entirety, while, in the other, we possess far the greater part of it.

The *Apology of Aristides* was, for ages, supposed to have finally perished, with a vast mass of the writings of antiquity.

Jerome, about the year 420, mentions the *Apology of Aristides*, and says that it was presented to the Emperor Hadrian at the same time with the *Apology of Quadratus*; that it was extant in his day, and was afterwards imitated by Justin Martyr. There is no later mention of its existence; but what has been called "a faint reflection" of the earlier testimony is found in the mediæval martyrologies as, in them, the 31st of August is given as the saints' day of "The blessed Aristides [to use the words of the old record] most renowned for faith and wisdom, who presented books on the Christian religion to the Prince Hadrian, and most brilliantly proclaimed in the presence of the emperor himself how that Christ Jesus is the only God."[1]

In the seventeenth century there was a rumor that the *Apology* was in some monastic libraries in Greece, but the search made for it was fruitless.

In the spring of the year 1889 Prof. J. Rendel Harris, the distinguished scholar and lecturer of Clare College, Cambridge, found, in the library of the St. Catherine Convent on Mount Sinai, where Tischendorf had thirty

---

[1] We find the *Apology* to be a powerful argument against polytheism and for the unity-in-trinity of God

years before discovered the *Codex Sinaiticus*, the long lost *Apology of Aristides*. It was in the Syriac language, in a manuscript which Prof. Harris refers to the sevènth century. Eleven years before this, the Mechitarist scholars in their convent of S. Lazaro, near Venice, had published a Latin translation of what was thought to be (and afterwards proved to be) the first two chapters of the *Apology* in the Armenian language. This fragment had been declared spurious by Renan and other scholars, because it contained a term describing the virgin as the "God-bearer"—a term which belonged to a much later age than that in which the *Apology of Aristides* was written. The original fragment was in the Armenian language, as has been said, and after fuller examination, the use of this term was found to have been due to a mistake of the Latin translator, and when Harris discovered the whole *Apology* in Syriac, this Armenian fragment was found to correspond with it, and its genuineness was vindicated. After the happy discovery of the *Apology* it was found, almost entire, in a slightly modified form, but in the original Greek, imbedded and concealed, like a jewel in common earth, in a strange story of the middle ages, entitled *Barlaam and*

Josaphat—a tale of such interest, in the absence of anything like the modern novel, that it was translated into some twenty languages, Hebrew and Icelandic being of the number. So seriously was the romance taken by the Church of Rome that Barlaam and Josaphat were accorded a place in the calendar of saints—a calendar, however, where much else equally as fictitious may be found.

The brilliant corypheus of the Ritschlians, Prof Adolf Harnack, in a notable article in the *Prussische Jahrbucher*, said : " The dis covery of this *Apology* is a find of the first importance." A glance at its contents will convince you that this is true. The *Apology of Aristides* is a witness not only for the gospels, but for the whole New Testament. The name New Testament occurs a little later, as we see from a quotation in Eusebius (H. E. v. 17).

III. THE APOLOGY AND THE NEW TESTAMENT

In examining the *Apology of Aristides* as to its dependence on the *New Testament*, there are several things to be considered. One is that it is brief, the translations of the Syriac and of the Greek, printed side by side in the

Ante-Nicene Fathers (Vol. IX) occupying only seventeen pages. The translation of the Greek, if complete, would occupy about seven pages. Of these seven pages, more than three-fourths of the space is occupied with arguments against the most prominent systems of polytheism, and for the unity-in-trinity of God. The arguments are chiefly philosophical, and are simply an appeal to reason. The emperor addressed was a heathen, supposed, as is shown, to know nothing of the writings of the Christians, which he is importuned again and again to read. Hence we should not expect quotations from these writings or any mention of the names of the writers—names which would be meaningless to Hadrian.

It will be in the interest of brevity and probably more satisfactory to the reader to refrain from a lengthened discussion, and present a sample of the *Apology*, the whole of which may not be accessible to some. Let us take the fifteenth section in which Aristides speaks of the origin of the Chistians, and refutes the heathen charges of immorality against them. We will take the translation from the Greek fragment as being probably more literal and briefer than the translation of the Syriac, which is itself a translation, and seemingly somewhat paraphrastic.[1] The first part—that about Christ—occurs earlier in the Syriac. "Now the Christians trace their origin from the Lord Jesus Christ, and he is acknowledged by the Holy Spirit to be the Son of the Most High God, who came down from heaven for the salvation of men, and being born of a pure virgin, unbegotten and immaculate, he assumed flesh and revealed himself among men that he might recall them to himself from their wandering after many gods. And having accomplished his wonderful dispensation, by a voluntary choice, he tasted death on the cross, fulfilling an august dispensation. And after three days he came to life again and ascended into heaven. And, if you would read, O King, you may judge the glory of his presence from the *holy gospel writing* as it is called among themselves. He had twelve disciples who, after his ascension, went forth into the provinces of the whole world, and declared his greatness. As for instance, one of them

---

[1] Dr J Armitage Robinson (now Dean of Westminster) edited the Greek text discovered by him in the story of Barlaam and Josaphat, as an appendix to Prof Rendel Harris's *Apology of Aristides*, in *Texts and Studies*, No 1 In introducing this appendix, Professor Harris says, in a spirit which is as beautiful as it is rare, "Need I say how gladly I make way for him in the appendix, which will really be the text itself."

Twin Lights from Athens 125

traversed the countries about us, proclaiming the doctrine of the truth. From this it is that they who still observe the righteousness enjoined by their preaching are called Christians.

"And these are they who more than all the nations on the earth have found the truth. For they know God the Creator and Fashioner of all things, through the only begotten Son and the Holy Spirit; and besides him they worship no other God. They have the commands of the Lord Jesus Christ himself graven upon their hearts; and they observe them, looking forward to the resurrection of the dead, and life in the world to come. They do not commit adultery nor fornication, nor bear false witness, nor covet the things of others; they honor father and mother, and love their neighbors; they judge justly, and they never do to others what they would not wish to happen to themselves,[1] they appeal to those

---

[1] The Syriac has, also, "and the food which is consecrated to idols they do not eat"

Dr. Purves has kindly drawn my attention to the indication in this *Apology* that the text of *The Acts* which Aristides used had at that time suffered correction. The negative form of the "golden rule" here seen is noted by Seeberg, of Berlin, as an instance of "Western" corruption of Acts 15 20 and 29, and Professor Harris, as is seen in his *Four Lectures on the Western Text*, agrees with him As this is found in connection with the statement that "they abstain

who injure them, and try to win them as friends; they are eager to do good to their enemies; they are gentle and easy to be entreated; they abstain from all unlawful conversation and from all impurity; they despise not the widow nor oppress the orphan; and he that has, gives ungrudgingly for the maintenance of him who has not. If they see a stranger they take him under their roof, and rejoice over him as over a very brother; for they call themselves brethren not after the flesh, but after the spirit."

When he tells the Emperor that one of the apostles "traversed the countries about us," we can hardly help believing that he refers to Paul, the apostle who first brought the gospel to Greece. Surely, too, it does not require a vivid imagination to hear, in the utterances of Aristides, echoes of Paul's address on Mars' Hill. While there are contrasts between the *Apology of Aristides* and this address, which we may call the *Apology of Paul*—contrasts

from εἰδωλοθυτα," Seeberg concluded that the interpretation was in the copy of *The Acts* used by Aristides. This would seem to indicate that *The Acts* was, as Seeberg says, "in ecclesiastical use," and that it was, even at that time, an "ancient book, handed down from the apostolic age."

My thanks are due to the Rev. T. W. Lingle, who kindly furnished me references from the *Four Lectures* to which I did not have access.

in which Professor Stokes, of Dublin, has seen a proof that *The Acts* was written in the first century—at the same time there are striking resemblances.[1] Let us look at some of them:—

Paul strove earnestly to make known to his heathen hearers "the unknown God." This we see Aristides tried to do for Hadrian, and in doing it, presented the theology—even the trinitarianism—of Paul's epistles.

Paul spoke of the folly of idolatry, and so does Aristides, with force and at length.

Paul spoke of the creation of "the world and all things therein," and so does Aristides.

Paul spoke of the resurrection, and so does Aristides. Paul spoke of the judgment, and of Christ as the Judge, and so does Aristides, in such words as these:—

"So shall they appear before the awful judgment, which through Jesus the Messiah, is destined to come upon the whole human race"

Paul speaks of the great mistakes of the Athenians in their worship, and declares of God that "he is Lord of heaven and earth" and that he "dwelleth not in temples made with hands; neither is worshiped with men's hands, as though he needed anything, seeing

[1] Expository New Testament, in loc.

he giveth to all life, and breath, and all things."
Paul was speaking to philosophers in Athens.
In the same Athens Aristides speaks of the
writers and philosophers among them, thus :—

"Herein, too, (they err) in asserting of deity
that any such thing as deficiency can be present to it, as when they say that he receives
sacrifice and requires burnt offering and
libation and immolations of men, and temples.
But God is not in need, and none of these
things are necessary to him."

When we remember that Paul's address to
the Epicurean and the Stoic philosophers occupied only ten verses of the seventeenth chapter
of The Acts, and when we see such correspondences in thought and even in diction between
the two "*Apologies*," can we resist the conviction that this passage of The Acts was in the
mind of Aristides, just as we have seen that
the fifteenth chapter was?

It is clear that the thought of Aristides
moved in the sphere of the gospels, The Acts,
the epistles and The Revelation, which constitute the New Testament. How could this
have been so, if what he calls "the holy gospel writing" and "their other writings" which
he exhorts the emperor to read, and from
which he says he derived his information, had

not been the same New Testament which we now have? It is perfectly safe to say that no objector can answer the question.

But besides this general mark of the identity of the truths proclaimed by Aristides with those of the New Testament, there is a remarkable coincidence in forms of expression, as for instance:—

Paul says (Col. 1: 17), "By him all things consist."

Aristides says, "Through him all things consist."

Paul says the heathen "served the creature more than the Creator."

Aristides says they "began to worship the creation more than their Creator."

James exhorts Christians to be "gentle, and easy to be entreated."

Aristides says, "They are gentle and easy to be entreated."

Paul speaks of the Jews as (Rom. 9: 3), "My brethren, my kinsmen according to the flesh."

And (Rom. 8: 5) uses the expression "not after the flesh, but after the Spirit."

Aristides says, "Brethren, not after the flesh, but after the Spirit."

Peter (2 Pet. 3: 16), speaking of the epistles of Paul, says: "As also in all his epistles

. . . in which are some things hard to be understood."

Aristides having told the emperor of "the holy gospel writing," says: "There are found in their other writings things which are hard to utter and difficult for one to narrate."[1]

In Hebrews (2:5; 6:5) we find the phrase, "the world to come."

Aristides speaks of those who seek "the world to come."

John in The Revelation (1:1) speaks of "the things which must come to pass (R. V.) hereafter," having already (1:19) received the command from the Saviour, "Write . . . the things which shall come to pass hereafter."

Aristides says, "Since I read in their writings, I was fully assured of these things as also of things which are to come."

Paul repeats God's promise, "I will put my laws into their hearts, and in their minds will I write them."

Aristides says the Christians "have the commands of the Lord Jesus Christ himself graven upon their hearts."

Paul exhorts Christians to give "not grudgingly"

---

[1] This expression "their other writings" occurs in the Syriac, but not in the Greek as we have it.

Twin Lights from Athens 131

Aristides says the Christian gives "ungrudgingly."

Peter (1 Pet. 1: 23) speaks of the regenerated as " born again, not of corruptible seed, but of incorruptible, by the word of God, which liveth and abideth forever."

Aristides says, "Let all that are without the knowledge of God, draw near there (*i e.*, to 'their doctrine'—'the gateway of light') and they will receive incorruptible words."

John, the beloved, says, "Let us love one another."

Aristides says, "And they love one another."

Further quotation would be wearisome, and, surely, is unnecessary. No one, unless under the influence of invincible prepossessions, could doubt that Aristides had read in what he refers to as "the gospel," "the Holy Gospel writing," as it is called among themselves, "their writings," "their other writings," just what we read in our New Testament These writings were not called the New Testament, as is well known, at first. But a writer against Montanism quoted by Eusebius (H. E v. 17) speaks of them in a way which shows that they were regarded as just as sacred as the most orthodox Christian considers them now. It seems clear, too, from his language that the book of The Revelation concluded the body of writings then, just as it does now. Speaking of opposing the doctrines of Montanus by arguments, he expresses himself as "apprehensive, lest, perhaps, I should appear to give any new injunctions, or to superadd anything to the doctrine of the New Testament, to which it is impossible that anything should be added or diminished by one who has resolved to live according to the gospel." "The gospel" and "their other writings" of Aristides must be the same body of writings called by this writer "the gospel" and "the New Testament," and the quotations given indicate that it was practically identical with the New Testament in our hands to-day.

Common sense demands an answer to this question:—

If these writings, evidently the same with our New Testament, were universally regarded by Christians in A. D. 125, as inspired and authoritative, and had been circulated all over the Roman world long before this and accepted everywhere as the sacred records of Christianity, how did they attain this universal acceptance in this character?

The only rational answer is that they went forth under apostolic authority. These writings, thus accepted by the great body of Christians, many thousands of whom were younger contemporaries of the Apostle John, must have had apostolic authorship or authorization. Any other explanation of their universal acceptance is irrational and incredible.

We have already found Justin Martyr imitating the illustrious example of his brother philosopher Aristides and presenting a more extended defense of the Christians to Antonine, the Pious, and his colleagues; and in this and the other writings of Justin we find him speaking also of "the gospel," giving it, or rather a part of it, another name, "*The Memoirs of the Apostles*" We have found that these contained what our four gospels do. Then we have seen standing by the side of Aristides at Athens in 125 a brave old man, presenting to Hadrian his defense of a somewhat different kind. This man had labored for Christ for a long term of service. He is of "the first immediate succession of the apostles," and had, not improbably, heard Paul preach, for he seems to have been a Roman; had the gift of prophecy, and is ranked with Agabus and the daughters of Philip; had seen some of those whom our blessed Lord had healed and raised from the dead; and this man had been one of those who had not only preached the gospel orally in many lands, but had distributed the written "Gospel" or New Testament including these "*Memoirs of the Apostles* and those that followed them." For, we know him as the fellow-apologist of Aristides, who, as we have seen, had these writings which Justin quotes so freely. We surely will not be asked to believe that Quadratus spent his life in distributing, as the authentic records of Christianity, gospels which were unauthorized by the apostles whom he immediately succeeded and whose work he, in company with others, took up. On the other hand he could not be supposed to have had a different set of Christian writings from those with which his companion apologist shows himself so familiar, and which bear so many marks of identity with those we have in our hands to-day.

In such witnesses as Justin, who sealed his testimony with his heart's blood, Aristides as courageous and faithful as his namesake who was surnamed "the Just," and Quadratus, who, true to his name, "stood four square to all the winds that blow," we have men whose evidence cannot lightly be brushed aside. As Professor Gildersleeve has said of the first, so we may say of all of them, "They were no holiday Christians."

Aristides told Hadrian that if he would read this "gospel," he would "perceive the power that belongs to it." All Christians experience this power; the history of the world clearly shows it too, and we could not but believe it to be true and divine, even if we knew nothing of its history; but it is a great gratification to be able to trace its utterances, by this and other lines, back to Christ and his apostles.

VI.

LIGHT FROM THE LAND OF THE PHARAOHS

EGYPTIAN darkness is a phrase with which we are all familiar; but in our day, from the land of the Pharaohs, where once fell a curse of "darkness which may be felt," and over which for centuries has hung a pall of ignorance, degradation and misery, much light is springing up. Not only is this light bursting forth from its great temples, and tombs of kings, but even the sands which cover long ruined towns and villages, and humbler burial-places, are yielding their torches for the illumination of the word of God. Even the specimens of "potsherd literature"—the *ostraka*, or inscribed pottery tablets—now found in large numbers and in many languages, and in many styles of writing, are adding their rays. Among them, some in Greek, are found to give remarkable confirmation to the accuracy of the New Testament.

But very clear light has been coming of late years from another source in the land of Egypt to dissipate the mists which unbelieving criticism has endeavored to throw round the New Testament, and the gospels especially. The book, *Supernatural Religion*, which served to unsettle the faith of so many Englishmen, had a very distinct echo from the shores of America. A learner who sat for years at the feet of its author—not literally, by going to England and receiving oral instruction, but by poring over the bulky three volumes here— has, in his turn, produced a book[1] by which many ill-informed Americans have been confirmed in infidelity.

The main contention of this book is that our four gospels were not written till "late in the second century," and that they were substituted, by ecclesiastical authority, for the original gospels, which were written in the first century, but are now lost. He tells his readers, "Of the numerous gospels which were in circulation in the second century, not more than three can with any certainty, or with any high degree of probability, be traced back to the time of the apostles. These are *The Gospel of Paul, The Gospel, or Recollections of Peter, and The Oracles, or Sayings, of Christ,* attributed to Matthew"

[1] "The History of the Christian Religion to the year 200," by C. B. Waite

The last-named, he thinks, assumed the form of the "*Gospel according to the Hebrews*," in a later development. He also conjectures that the *Gospel according to the Egyptians* was a version of it.

Now as to *The Gospel of Paul*, I think there need be no discussion. When Paul used the words, "according to my gospel," the connection shows that he meant the Gospel of Christ as preached by him, and not a gospel which he had written. This is too puerile to notice further. The author does not venture to assert that there is any trace of the existence, at any time, of such a writing in the form of even a single quotation from it; though he ventures to guess that it was perpetuated, in its first stage of evolution, in *The Gospel of Marcion*. "It may be inferred," he tells us, "that it afterwards became incorporated in *The Gospel of Marcion*, A. D., 145."

The *Oracles, or sayings*, of Christ, if they existed,[1] are "lost," indeed, as he says, but the *Gospel according to the Hebrews*, which the author thinks is its secondary form, is not wholly lost. Twenty-three fragments are

---

[1] No trace of such a writing, distinct from the Gospel of Matthew, can be found

preserved, and these we have the right to examine. What is the result? In this heretical writing, the traces of our four gospels are plainly visible,[1] showing, of course, their previous existence. *The Gospel according to the Hebrews* was evidently a reconstruction of the four gospels, with certain additions and changes to furnish a support for the peculiar views of the Judaizing sect of the Ebionites. This sect seems to have had predecessors in some churches even before the death of the Apostle John, and may be referred to by him in the Apocalypse as those " who say they are Jews, and are not, but do lie," and whom he describes as "of the synagogue of Satan." Their heretical gospel, with which they tried to supplant the four gospels, may have been written very early in the second century; and if so, as even the few fragments which remain show that our gospels were all drawn upon, the fact that these gospels were written before the close of the first century is an almost necessary inference; for such use of them indicates that they were not only already written, but that they were the accepted and authorized foundations of Christian belief, and

[1] See Dr B. Weiss' Introduction to N. T., Vol II, § 45, 5.

no one can imagine that they could be extensively copied, distributed, and accepted as authoritative in a moment.

While the writer of this new view of the early history of the Christian religion thinks that our *Gospel of Luke* was a late second century evolution from his imaginary *Gospel of Paul*, and Matthew another, from the *Gospel according to the Hebrews*, he makes, the, for him, very unfortunate guess that the Gospel of Mark is a second century edition of the *Gospel of Peter*, which he has classed among the original first century gospels.

Unfortunately for this hypothesis, a considerable part of the *Gospel according to Peter* has been discovered; and a translation of the fragment by the distinguished scholar, Canon J. Armitage Robinson, editor of Cambridge Texts and Studies, lies before me. It was discovered by the French Archæological Mission, Cairo, in 1886 at Akhmim[1] (Panopolis) in Upper Egypt, in a grave, supposed to be that of a monk. It is a parchment manuscript, and is thus described:—

"The Akhmim manuscript, six by four and three-fourth inches in size, is written in uncial characters, in a sloping hand current in manu-

[1] Written, also, Akhmin.

scripts of the seventh to the ninth century, and contains on thirty-three vellum leaves (sixty-six pages) the *Gospel according to Peter*, and the *Apocalypse of Enoch*."

The author of this so-called *History of the Christian Religion to the Year 200* holds that these three Gospels—of Paul, of Peter, and according to the Hebrews—were "suppressed" by the strong hand of ecclesiastical authority, and that our four gospels—of later origin, in his opinion—were "substituted" for them. As an actual instance of such suppression and substitution, he quotes from Eusebius' Ecclesiastical History, Book VI, Ch. 12, where is preserved part of a letter of Serapion, bishop of Antioch, written in A. D. 190, to the Church of Rhossus in Cilicia, which was under his care. It seems that some of the people there were taken with the Gospel of Peter, of which their bishop seems to have known nothing before this. As soon as Serapion became aware of the character of this so-called "Gospel," he condemned it as unfit to be used, because it had evidently been forged in the interest of the Docetæ,[1] a heretical sect to

---

[1] That is Seemers—people who taught that Christ had not really become a man, but only seemed to do so, assuming, not a real, but a phantasmal human body.

which the Apostle John seems clearly to refer when he speaks of some who denied that "Jesus Christ had come in the flesh."

This author tells us:—

"In the year 190, a large number of these Gospels of Peter were found in use by the Church of Rhossus in Cilicia; and so much were the Christians of that church attached to them that it became necessary for Serapion to suppress them and substitute the canonical gospels in their stead."

Now let us lay this statement and the facts of the case as stated in Eusebius side by side, and see how they agree. Here is a part of Serapion's letter:—

"We, brethren, receive Peter and the other apostles even as Christ; but the writings that go falsely by their name we reject, as we are well acquainted with them, and know also that we have not received such handed down to us." . . . He tells them that he became acquainted with the character of this so-called gospel by borrowing it from some "whom we called Docetæ, for most of its views are those of this sect."

The author of this remarkable "history" is said to be a judge; but for a judge, he deals strangely with the evidence before him.

Where does he learn that the four gospels were "substituted" for this Gospel of Peter when it was suppressed? Neither Eusebius nor Serapion tells of any such substitution; and all, except those prepossessed with the author's theory, would understand that Serapion forbade the use of this *Gospel of Peter*—which he calls a forgery—along with the "received" gospels, which they evidently used already, as nothing is said about substituting them in the place of the forbidden one which went falsely under the name of Peter.

Sometimes, in looking up from my writing, I see, on a ridge a half-mile or so away, an electric car rapidly crossing the field of vision, and at certain points, behaving in a strange way. Sometimes it will be suddenly elongated, and then, as quickly shortened. Again its whole shape will change, and then it will suddenly rear up as if to jump a hurdle, and then as quickly plunge downward as if about to bury itself in the earth. Is the car actually thus eccentric and frolicsome? Of course I know that it is not, for I have often ridden on it over that very place and know that the rails are straight and smooth, and that the cars behave themselves decently. I know that the pranks of which this one seems to be guilty are only apparent: in short that the whole series of strange antics is the result of inequalities in the glass of the window through which I look. It is all due to the waves and bubbles in the glass; their effect being magnified by the distance. The medium through which we view a thing has much to do with the notion we get of it. Our judge has looked at this testimony through the medium of his suppression—and—substitution theory.

The question as to which were the original writings in this case is no longer a subject for guessing The discovery of the fragment of the *Gospel according to Peter* makes this plain. We have the testimony of such a scholar as Dr. Sanday of Oxford University, for instance, to this effect:—

"The apocryphal *Gospel of Peter* is based upon our gospels" (see his Bampton Lectures, especially p. 301, note). He gives a number of instances in which terms peculiar to the four gospels are used in this *Gospel according to Peter*, besides other evidences of its dependence on them; and, referring to the heretical changes and additions in this so-called gospel, says of the author of it: "It is very plain where he begins to walk by himself." Referring to these eccentric features of the forgery he says: "In all these ways the contrast between the apocryphal gospel and the canonical gospels is marked. The latter are really 'a garden inclosed.' Intrusive elements seem to be carefully kept out of them. They preserve the type of language, as it can be abundantly shown, that they also preserve the type of idea, which was appropriate just to the three years of our Lord's public ministry, and no more."

Other testimonies might be given, but they can hardly be necessary. The writer of the introduction of the *Gospel according to Peter* in the Ante-Nicene Fathers (volume IX), though evidently not a conservative, does not even raise the question as to the originality of our gospels. His only question is as to whether the forged writing does not draw its materials from other sources besides our gospels. He concludes that, " whether the author used any other sources than the canonical gospels is a matter still in doubt."

But the *Gospel according to Peter itself*, if space could be allowed to introduce it, would furnish the most convincing proof the intelligent reader could ask that it drew its materials from all four of the canonical gospels.

Now we all know that materials must exist before the manufactured article—the wool before the cloth, the cloth before the coat.

When we apply the facts, as they now stand in the clear light of discovery, to the theory of our author, something takes place very much like the vanishing into airy nothingness of a brilliant, big bubble when pricked with a pin.

So enamored is the author of this "history" with his theory of suppression—and—substitution that he leaves his period of the first two centuries, and like a heedless boy, chases his bubble down through the centuries to the fifth, where while he imagines it most beautiful, it suddenly bursts as he is admiring its iridescent glories. He tells us (p. vii. Fifth Ed.):—

"The fact is, there are various instances of the displacement of older gospels and the substitution of the canonical in their stead. Even as late as the fifth century Theodoret found it necessary to suppress the Gospel of Tatian and substitute in its place the four gospels"

He then quotes Theodoret, as we have already done. "I found, myself," says Theodoret, (A. D 430) "upwards of two hundred such books held in honor among your churches, and collecting them all together, I laid them aside, and instead, introduced the gospels of the four evangelists." On page 326, fifth edition, the author expresses the opinion that "The fact that Theodoret felt obliged to suppress it is inconsistent with the theory that it is a harmony of the four gospels."

We all know the truth now. It *is* a harmony of the four gospels, and could not have been older than they, just as the cloth cannot be older than the wool of which it is woven, or the coat than the cloth of which it is made. The four gospels were the materials out of which the *Diatessaron of Tatian* (*i. e.*, as the word means, the "through four"—four gospels, or four evangelists) was made.

The discovery of the *Diatessaron of Tatian* was to the main contention of the Tübingen School like the stone from David's sling to the forehead of Goliath. Honest scholars, formerly of that school, acknowledge that discoveries have now demonstrated the falsity of the opinion of Baur and his followers that the gospels were not written till the second century. We have already seen the conclusions of that brilliant leader, Prof. Adolf Harnack of Berlin; and no honest man who knows the facts will try to stand by the contention of this author that our gospels were written "late in the second century." There may be exceptions in the case of those who though, like him, not conscious of intentional dishonesty, yet have their vision so warped by theories that they are incapable of seeing facts as they are. In his edition of 1900, published several years after the discoveries, mentioned in this little book, were made, he fails to mention them.

But we should not judge him too harshly. He is human, and it could not have been an agreeable task to record facts so destructive of his theory. Then, too, they would undeceive so may of his readers. Ignorance is the mother of infidelity, as well as of superstitious devotion.

In the preface to the third edition of this work, republished in the fifth edition, on page seven the author says:—

"In conclusion, we again call attention to the fact that none of the main propositions of this work have been in the slightest degree impeached; much less, overthrown."

It is to be hoped that the author will not repeat this in future editions. Should he do so, after being informed of the facts which have been mentioned, his professions of candor will fall under something more than suspicion.¹

The Gospel according to Peter and *the Gospel according to the Hebrews*, not only show that our four gospels were already in existence when they were written, and thus are valuable witnesses for them, but they tend to confirm them in another way. The *character* of these productions stands in marked contrast to that of the four gospels. As soon as they leave the support of our gospels and begin "to walk by themselves," we see with what tottering and wayward footsteps they proceed. When we read the account of the resurrection of Christ in the *Gospel according to Peter*, we find it declaring of those who were guarding the tomb, "Again they see three men come forth from the tomb, and

---

¹ It may be thought that too much has been said about the two books, *Supernatural Religion*, and *The History of the Christian Religion to the Year Two Hundred*, but as these are the two chief efforts of infidelity in our times, the one in England and the other in America, and as the light of discovery has so strikingly revealed their falsity, the course pursued has seemed to me to be the true one Besides this, mere references to infidelity in general can hardly be so satisfactory to any truth seeker as the presentation of particular facts which furnish a refutation of particular claims of infidelity The concrete is more impressive than the abstract—the particular than the general.

three of them supporting one, and a cross following them: and of the two the head reached unto the heaven, but the head of him that was led by them overpassed the heavens. And they heard a voice from the heavens, saying, 'Thou hast preached unto them that sleep.' And a response was heard from the cross, 'Yea!'" We look at the fragments of the *Gospel according to the Hebrews*, and find one of them representing our Saviour as speaking of the Holy Spirit as his 'Mother,' and as taking him by one hair of his head and transporting him to a distant mountain. We find ourselves, here, in a different region from that of the gospels. We observe a tone altogether different from theirs, and recognize in the strange atmosphere, mephitic odors of something so akin to blasphemy and sacrilege, that we feel the disposition to rush away to escape asphyxia.

As a recent writer[1] has well said:—

"The simplicity, directness and conciseness of the four is gone; their doctrinal purity is departed; we are now in the realm of haggada."

Canon Armitage Robinson, the translator,

[1] Rev. R B Woodworth in *Presbyterian Quarterly* for January, 1895

(as quoted by the same author) says of the results of the examination of the *Gospel according to Peter :—*

"The facts are just as they should be if the church's universal tradition as to the supreme and unique position of the four canonical gospels is still to be sustained by historical criticism. The words of Irenæus (A. D. 200) are as true as ever to-day, and they have received a new and notable confirmation by our latest recovery: 'So strong is the position of our gospels that the heretics themselves bear witness to them, and each must start from them to prove his own doctrine.'"

We have already seen that, when Ciasca showed the Apostolic Visitor of the Catholic Copts the manuscript of the *Diatessaron* in the Vatican library, this ecclesiastic told him of another in Egypt in the possession of Ghalim Dos Ghali, the Copt, "the Catholic"; and that it was presented to the Apostolic See and deposited in the Borgian library. This manuscript, being complete, supplied what was missing in the other, and having a better text, was useful in correcting it. Thus Egypt contributed additional brightness to the rays of the "great light from the Vatican."

But, besides those already named, there are other lights from the land of the Pharaohs.

In July, 1897, two young Oxford scholars, Messrs. Grenfel and Hunt, were engaged in explorations on the edge of the Lybian desert, some 130 miles south of Cairo, on the site of the old city of Oxyrrhynchus, once a place of considerable size, as its ruins show, and an important Christian center in the early centuries of our era. They made many literary discoveries among the rubbish heaps of the old city, and one of these has been the subject of much comment and speculation among Christian scholars. It was a leaf from a papyrus book containing Logia, or sayings, of our Lord. In it we discover, at once, an echo of the sayings of our Lord in the gospels; and one of them is identical with a saying recorded in Luke. Experts say that " the papyrus was probably written not later than the year 200." While one sentence corresponds with one in Luke, others, in words used, or in the sentiments expressed, suggest both Matthew's and John's Gospels as sources. But along with what is familiar, there is much that is novel and not a little obscure in these "sayings." Reading them and trying, with all one's might, to understand some of them, makes one thank-

Light from the Land of the Pharaohs 153

ful that our gospels recorded our Saviour's "sayings" before they were twisted, unintentionally, or intentionally, for the support of some theory, into forms which are false, as we see in the apocryphal gospels of heretical sects, or were shrouded with Delphic obscurity, as we find them in some of the Oxyrrhynchus Logia.

Near this Logia fragment, there were discovered remains of Homer's *Iliad and Odyssey*, of Thucydides and other classical writers; but, what is of most interest to us, papyrus leaves containing seven verses of the Epistle to the Romans, two pages of the Gospel of John, and a leaf of the Gospel of Matthew were found. The fragment of the Gospel according to John is thus spoken of by the Secretary of the Egyptian Exploration Fund, Dr. W. C. Winslow:—

"The fragment of St. John's Gospel forms an important portion, small though it be, of a book of about fifty pages containing that gospel, dating about 200. We have St. John 1: 23–41, except that verse thirty-two is wanting: also St. John 20: 11–25, except that verse eighteen is missing." After further describing it, he says, "The papyrus belongs to the same class with the Vatican and Sinaitic

Codices," and that it "is a remarkable corroboration of those texts and of our accepted version."

The fragment of Romans is in large uncial characters rather rudely made, and is thought to be a schoolboy's exercise; and if this be true it is an additional indication of the extensive use of the New Testament at its date of A. D. 316.

But the most interesting of these finds at Oxyrrhynchus is a papyrus leaf containing a part of the first chapter of Matthew.

Dr. Winslow says:—

"Its date is fixed by some experts at A. D. 150, and by the editors of the society's publications at fifty or sixty years later."

The Greek text seems to be almost absolutely identical with that of Westcott and Hort on which our Revised Version is founded. Prof. Rendel Harris, by a very close examination, thinks he has discovered an apostrophe which this revised Greek text does not show; but one is tempted to ask whether this little mark might not have been due to some minute speck on the papyrus. The identity is about as nearly absolute as would be possible in copying one page of Greek from another. Indeed a copyist would have to make a good many

Light from the Land of the Pharaohs 155

trials before he could reproduce a page of Greek as perfectly. This is very remarkable. Here are two Greek texts, between the writing of which probably seventeen centuries have rolled away, and yet they are practically identical. This tends to confirm what was said by Dr. Hort long before this discovery:—

"If comparative trivialities, such as changes of order, the omission or insertion of an article with proper names, and the like, are set aside, the words" (in the Greek Testament) "in our opinion still subject to doubt can hardly amount to a thousandth part of the whole New Testament."

In transcribing the vast number of copies which we now have, a great multitude of mistakes was unavoidable; but the great number of copies enables us to see what the mistakes were in any one copy. This has brought it about that the text of the New Testament is now in a state of certainty which far surpasses that of the Greek or Latin classics that have come down to us.[1] This leaf of Matthew, probably the oldest scrap of writing containing a page of the Greek New Testament is a bright light from the land of the Pharaohs, showing the fixedness of the text and its pres-

[1] See Appendix.

ervation in purity to our own times, in spite of the inevitable mistakes of copyists, and the efforts of heretics to corrupt it. To all theories of the gradual evolution of the New Testament from mere germs to its present form, it gives a death-blow, a veritable *coup de grace.*

VII.

MANY LIGHTS FROM MANY LANDS, OR LIGHT ON THE SETTING

SOME years ago there was found on the Acropolis at Athens, built into a long-buried wall, a slab of marble on which appeared, in relief, a female head. The archæologist in charge of excavations which were in progress, M. Kavvadias, pronounced it a fragment of the frieze of Phidias on the Parthenon near at hand. Other archæologists thought this improbable. After much discussion, an artist recollected that, among the specimens of the Parthenon frieze among the Elgin marbles in the British Museum, there was a group in which appeared a female figure—that of Iris, the goddess of the rainbow—without a head. A cast was taken from the broken slab discovered on the Acropolis, and sent to England. Parts of the slab had been broken away, possibly by a mason's hammer in fitting it into the wall, so that, in those parts, it did not fit the missing place in the frieze; but it was necessary only to put the fragment into the vacant place to see that it belonged there. Protuberances and corresponding depressions in the marble just fitted, and a lifted arm and hand on the frieze met with long-lost fingers holding the twist of hair at the back of the head—the head of Iris, the rainbow goddess.

The sight of such a correspondence flashes conviction more quickly than reasoning, and leads to a conclusion more reliable than the most labored arguments of the most distinguished experts.

Something like this has occurred in the case of the New Testament.

When we find, in any writing, incidental references to passing events, to political conditions, to methods of governmental administration, to names of official positions and of persons occupying them, to geographical features and names of places, to peculiar customs among the people described, we have an indication that the writer had personal knowledge of these particulars which only one living in the period of these occurrences would be likely to have. If he implies that he lives in the time of which he writes, and if the most searching investigations show more and more plainly, as they are pursued, that his representations of all these particulars are correct, we never doubt that the accounts are given by a contemporary writer, unless thoroughly convincing evidence is adduced to prove that he has made a false claim.

If several writings, very different from each other in their style of composition and general character, which have always been attributed to *different* writers, speak from various points of view of the same general subject, and all have, in various degrees, these incidental references in them, then, it must be admitted that the improbability that the accounts originated at a later period is greatly increased. Such a conspiracy for deception, without any imaginable motive, would be well-nigh incredible; and the amount of research to be undertaken by each individual to avoid mistakes would present a task before which even the archæological expert would quail.

With our habits of travel and means of rapid transit, with our newspapers, magazines, reviews, and archæological publications, we can hardly estimate the difficulty of such an undertaking on the part of any writers of the second century to reproduce all the particulars of the situation of the first, as they are incidentally, naturally, and without effort presented in the writings of the New Testament.

Now, if we had been at the British Museum when the plaster cast of the head of Iris was brought from Athens, and had merely seen that, when put in the place of the frieze where a head was missing, the size of the head was as it should be, and that the pose of the statue was correct, that the outline of the fragment fitted the outline of the vacant space on the frieze, and especially, if we saw that the fingers on the head grasping the lock of hair just met an arm and hand that fitted them, on the frieze, we would ask no further proof that this fragment was the long lost head of Iris. There might be a thousand lines and angles to correspond with a thousand lines and angles in the broken surface on the frieze, yet we would not wait to have each one of these calculated by mathematical processes. The fitting as we saw it would be as thoroughly convincing as volumes of mathematical calculations.

Volumes might be, and have been, written on the correspondences of the New Testament and its setting; but the presentation of a very few of the multitude of particulars will be sufficiently convincing.

These correspondences, however, are so

numerous that we experience an *embarras des richesses*. It is hard to select from them; but we may as well begin at the beginning. In connection with the account of the birth of our blessed Lord, Luke tells us that in obedience to a decree of Augustus Cæsar commanding a universal "enrollment" in the Roman Empire, Joseph and Mary, being descendants of King David, went to their "own city," Bethlehem, to be enrolled, and that this enrollment took place while Cyrenius (Latin, Quirinus) was governor of Syria. Two objections have been raised to the truthfulness of this statement. One is the assertion that Cyrenius did not become governor of Syria till several years after our Saviour's birth. But the meaning may be that the decree, though *issued* earlier, only became completely *effective* (ἐγενετο) in all parts of the province during the governorship of Cyrenius. But another more probable explanation is in the fact that "there has been no serious refutation of the view first developed by Zumpt that Quirinus was twice governor of Syria."[1]

The second objection was that there was no record of such an enrollment earlier than the

[1] Maclear's Historical Illustrations of the New Testament Scriptures.

reign of the Emperor Nero. But recent discoveries by Messrs. Grenfel and Hunt at Oxyrrhynchus in Egypt have thrown new light on this subject. "The important matter is that we are now for the first time put in possession of contemporary confirmation of Luke's statement that 'there went out a decree from Cæsar Augustus, that all the world should be enrolled.' . . .

"The one point that may now be considered as settled by Messrs. Grenfel and Hunt's discovery is that the first census ordered by Augustus certainly occurred in the time of Herod" (*Biblia*, December, 1899).

So the objection is turned into a confirmation. We now see the birth of our blessed Lord linked not only with the administration of the great world-ruler and of his representative in the province of Syria, but with a definite and far-reaching act of that administration which was repeated at regular intervals by his successors. The decree of Augustus is now plainly seen to be not an invention of Luke but a fact of history.

The fact stated by Luke (2: 3) that in Judæa each person went to his "own city" to be enrolled, also throws a sidelight on the peculiarity of the application of Roman government to

Jewish customs which must appeal to all who are informed and are capable of thinking. It is most suggestive of the peculiar customs of the Jews and of the wise rule of Rome to avoid all unnecessary antagonism with existing customs and institutions among nations under her control.

The return from Egypt furnishes another view, in Matthew's description of it, of the political status of Judæa soon after the death of Herod the Great. Why was Joseph "afraid" to return to Judæa when he heard that Archelaus reigned in the room of his father Herod?

The fact that this young monster turned loose his soldiery on the people and slew three thousand of them, soon after he assumed control, in the precincts of the temple itself, suggests a reason. Why did he consider Nazareth in Galilee a safer place of abode? The fact that Herod Antipas ruled there and that the power of Archelaus was confined to Judæa explains this.

These facts connected with the birth and infancy of our Lord as stated by these two evangelists are but samples of a vast number of incidental references which show the perfect familiarity of the writers of the New Testament with the political status in the

Holy Land during these times. The political conditions of the period covered by the New Testament narrative were such that no writer could have forged the accounts at a later time without falling into many mistakes. The government of the country was administered in five distinct forms during this period. Even the astute, careful and clear-headed Tacitus, writing near the end of the first century, and doubtless with access to public records, seems to have been unable successfully to thread the mazes of a situation so complicated; and the most skillful forger who, in the second century, should have attempted the telling of such a story as that of the gospels and The Acts would have tripped at every step. How is it with the New Testament writers? Here is the answer of one who has examined the facts very carefully:—

"The writers of the New Testament nowhere betray any perplexity. They mark quite incidentally, and without the slightest trace of strain or effort, the various phases, extraordinary as they were, of the civil government of Palestine. Thus, at the era of the advent we find (1) the whole country subject to the sole rule of Herod the Great (Matt. 2:1; Luke 1:5); then (2) we have his dominions parti-

Many Lights from Many Lands 165

tioned out among his sons, while one, Archelaus, rules over Judæa with the title of king (Matt. 2:22); then (3) we see Judæa reduced to the condition of a Roman province, while Galilee,Ituræa and Trachonitis continue under native princes (Luke 3:1); then (4) in the person of Herod Agrippa I, we have the old kingdom of Palestine restored (Acts 12:1); and finally (5) we observe the whole country, reduced under Roman rule and Roman procurators (Felix, Acts 23:24; Festus, Acts 24:27), while a certain degree of deference is paid to Herod Agrippa II, to whom Festus refers Paul's case as presenting special difficulties."[1]

But this is only the vestibule I will not attempt to exhibit in detail the many complications which would have furnished snares and pitfalls for any forger who might have attempted, in the second century, to write such accounts The writer just quoted has summed up the difficulties which such an attempt would have encountered under five heads:—

1. The political condition of Palestine—just mentioned.
2. Roman emperors and administrators.
3. Jewish kings and princes.
4. Condition of the Jewish nation.

[1] Maclear's Historical Illustrations.

5. The Greek and Roman world.

Under each of these heads, as every reader must know, there is an intricate array of particulars. This makes it plain, not only that the task of the forger of the second century would have been an impossible one, but that the subject is too large to pursue further in this direction.

The Holy Land itself is a witness to the truth of the narratives in the gospels so far as testimony of such a character can be confirmatory. The land as it now lies, after all the changes of centuries effected by Romans, Saracens, Crusaders, the deadening hand of the Turk, and the great forces of nature operating on its unprotected surface for almost two millenniums, is still so striking as the scene and setting of the wonderful story that it has been called the Fifth Gospel. Modern surveys, explorations and excavations are continually adding to our knowledge of the almost innumerable correspondences between the Land and the Book. Just before writing this there has come under my eye the announcement of the identification of Bethabara where John the Baptist baptized on the Jordan, at the southern end of the Lake of Galilee—a discovery which clears up difficulties in the narrative created by the location of the traditional site; and new discoveries, tested by the application of scientific principles, and freed from the delusions of legend, are continually contributing to our knowledge of "those holy fields" (as said the dying king centuries ago),

> "Over whose acres walked those blessed feet
> Which, fourteen hundred years ago, were nailed
> For our advantage, on the bitter cross"

The journeys and experiences of the Apostle Paul, as related in The Acts and referred to in his Epistles, find a no less striking confirmation in the setting of each incident as seen in the light of modern discovery.

Wood's discoveries at Ephesus[1] have thrown a flood of light on the account of Paul's experiences there as given in the nineteenth chapter of The Acts.

From the accounts of Ephesus given by historians, especially by Pliny and Strabo, and from coins and inscriptions and the revelations of exploration, it is now easy to see why the temple of Diana (Artemis) of the Ephesians was reckoned one of the seven wonders of the world, and why anything which seemed to

[1] *Discoveries at Ephesus*, by J. T. Wood, F S. A, London, 1877.

threaten interests connected with the worship conducted in this marvel of architecture, which was, at once, the chief shrine and treasury of western Asia, might naturally arouse such a tumult as that which Luke describes, and lead to the gathering of the great assemblage in that vast theater whose remains indicate that twenty thousand people could be seated there. The mention of the "silver shrines of Diana," the "no small gain" of the "craftsmen" engaged in this manufacture, "the temple of the great goddess Diana," and "her magnificence," the indication of the wide extent of the cult—"whom all Asia and the world worshipeth"—the rushing "with one accord into the theater," the expressions, "town clerk" (grammateus), "the city of the Ephesians is the worshiper (neokoros—temple-sweeper) of the great Goddess Diana," "the image which fell down from Jupiter," deputies (anthupatoi), "lawful assembly" (ecclesia), all occurring in the space of twelve verses, present to us unique features of an occurrence of which Ephesus, as history and archæology combine in showing it to have been, was the scene, and the only possible scene in all the world. No jewel ever fitted its setting more perfectly.

When we go back and see Paul in Macedonia

Many Lights from Many Lands 169

we find similar correspondences between the narrative of Luke and the environment in each place as history and recent discovery present it.

For instance, Philippi is said to be (Acts 16:12) "the chief city of that part of Macedonia, and a colony." The word translated "part" is a peculiar one as here used, and the following throws new light on it:—

"In Chapter XVI, which contains an account of Paul's visit to Philippi in Macedonia, a word is used (Meris) to designate the 'district' in Macedonia in which it was situated, which occurs nowhere else in that signification, so that its genuineness has been justly suspected. But among the Fayum documents a considerable number make use of just the same word to describe divisions in that region." The account shows us, too, all the accompaniments of a "colony"—that peculiar institution of the Roman Empire, entirely different from a colony in the modern sense—by which cities in different provinces of the empire, for some special service, were honored with the title, privileges and form of government which made them Romes in miniature.

At Thessalonica we find companions of Paul brought before "the rulers of the city" (Gr. Politarchai). This peculiar name is said not to occur in any other place in Greek literature. Yet an arch only recently demolished in Thessalonica (now Salonika) bore an inscription which stated that it was erected when certain persons, whose names are given, were "politarchs of the city."

We may not tarry with Paul at Athens to study the vivid portrayal of the scene in which he stands among the Stoics and Epicureans to preach the gospel of Christ, but we can obtain an instructive glimpse through the very intelligent eyes of another. Prof. Ernst Curtius of the University of Berlin, the great Greek scholar and historian, said in the "Reports of the Royal Academy of Sciences" in 1893; under the title Paulus in Athens:—

"Whoever approaches the report as given in The Acts without pre-judgments and in fairness, cannot, in my conviction, do otherwise than accept the account as that of a well-informed and truthful witness." After giving his grounds for this belief, he says:—

"I can only conclude as I began, that it is my firm conviction that whoever denies the historical character of the report of Paul in Athens tears out of the history of mankind one of its most important pages."

When we retrace our steps again, and find

Paul in Paphos on the island of Cyprus, we are on the scene of another triumph of the truth. Luke gives the governor, Sergius Paulus, the title anthupatos (translated "deputy" in King James' version), and the accusation of inaccuracy was made against his account; but besides the statement of Dio Cassius showing that he was correct, a coin of Cyprus and an extended inscription, both of the reign of Claudius, have been discovered, containing the names of persons who were proconsuls, and with this title, anthupatos, on them, thus fully vindicating Luke's accuracy.

These are but samples of almost innumerable correspondences that might be mentioned, but it is hoped that they are sufficient.

There were parts broken away from the outer edges of the fragment of marble bearing the bas-relief of a female head and fingers of a hand, and a very hardy objector might say that we do not know that, if preserved, they would have fitted into the still vacant spaces on the frieze. Ordinary mortals, however, would feel perfectly sure, from the perfect fitting of that which was found, that these little fragments, if found, would fit into their places, too. Just so the general and perfect fitting of the New Testament into its environment, so far as it has been determined by the strictest scientific methods—a fitting becoming more evident with each new discovery—goes to confirm the conclusion that, could that environment be perfectly known, the correspondence would be perfect. The fitting of the head of Iris to her body on the Pentelic marble of the frieze is hardly more convincing of the fact that it belongs there than are the facts at which we have been looking, that the New Testament belongs to its traditional setting, the apostolic age.

We have seen many lights falling on the New Testament, all combining to make clear the fact that it was not written in the second century, from uncertain traditions, but in the first, by men who were thoroughly informed about the great facts of the redemption through Christ. We have more accurate and detailed contemporary testimony, by thoroughly competent witnesses, about Christ than about any other historical character of ancient times. It would be more rational to doubt that Julius Cæsar laid the foundation of the Roman Empire than that Christ founded that greater empire, the Kingdom of Heaven. With the progress of discovery, light after light has risen to shine on the New Testament, each adding to the evidence of the reliableness of its record; but the clearest light of all is not that which shines upon it, but that which shines from it—the portraiture of him who is the light of the world.

He is no shadowy being encompassed with a mist of legend, but a clearly drawn historical character, yet entirely unique, rising infinitely beyond any other the world has ever seen; who, though he lived a public life of only about three years, and never led an army or wrote a book, has, yet, influenced the human race as no other man or set of men can be claimed to have done. With Jean Paul Richter, we see in him that One, " who, being the holiest among the mighty, the mightiest among the holy, lifted, with his pierced hand, empires off their hinges and turned the stream of the centuries out of its channel, and still governs the ages."

These grand words impress us with the greatness of a Being, who, though a man, has no equal. The mightiest, the holiest, because he is God as well as man. But without divine inspiration, even genius cannot venture to describe Christ except in general terms. Genius can give us but a glimpse of the glorious personality—yea, can but touch the outer fringe of his robe. Whenever men, uninspired, endeavor to give the detailed portrait of Christ, they always fail. There is always some act, some expression, some tone in the utterance, that is out of keeping with the Christ we find portrayed in the New Testament.

Indeed, it seems impossible for mere human genius to depict even a merely human ideal. George Eliot, with all her wonderful insight into character and skill in presenting it to her readers, yet fails when she tries to paint perfection. Her Daniel Deronda is a failure, because she tried to represent him as faultless.[1] The result has been described, on account of the indefiniteness of the portraiture, as a "moral mist" instead of a man.

How different it is with the writers of the New Testament! They do not deal in mere generalities and indefinite expressions such as lifting empires off their hinges, and turning the stream of the centuries They do not merely tell us that he is the holiest and the mightiest, but let us see him doing deeds and speaking words and exhibiting a spirit, which make us feel that he is. While they never satisfy a vulgar curiosity about his person—

[1] The Church's One Foundation, pp. 94, 95.

never even giving a hint about his personal appearance—yet they tell us definitely what he did, what he said, and sometimes, with what gesture or look he spoke. We catch utterances of the greatest beauty and sublimity and force, and yet never think of him as merely a great poet or great orator. He exhibits the highest order of courage, endurance, and self-command, and yet we never think of him as merely the greatest of heroes. He does deeds and speaks words of unspeakable kindness, and yet we never think of him as merely the greatest philanthropist. We always feel, as we look at this portraiture on the pages of the evangelists, that there is in him something far, yea infinitely, above all this. When we behold him a new-born infant we feel that we must bow in worship with the wise men and the shepherds. When we see him as a youth, with the doctors, we cannot but wonder at his wisdom; and in the synagogue at Nazareth, the wonder at the gracious words which proceeded out of his mouth, which his own townsfolk felt, is still felt by us as we read. Whether with authority, he teaches the people, or with unflinching courage, exposes and rebukes the hypocrisy of the scribes and Pharisees, or with tenderness, forgives the woman who was a sinner, or in lowliness, receives sinners and eats with them, or stoops to wash his disciples' feet, we feel that here is one different from all other men. Whether we see him calming the sea, or filling the net with fishes, or feeding the multitudes, or recalling the dead to life, or bearing the stripes and the thorn-crowning, or hanging on the cross, or rising from the tomb, or ascending to his Father, our hearts thrill with the impulse to adore, to worship, to love and serve him. It is this impulse, not momentary, but lasting through the ages, that sends the missionaries across the seas and makes martyrs endure torture and death—that nerved a Paul to work and suffer and die in the first century, and Chinese Christians in the end of the nineteenth.

Well might Irenæus speak of these writings as those "in which Christ is enthroned," and well may Robertson Nicoll say that "what is needed is that we should find out for ourselves, in patient study, the Christ of the gospels, not the Christ of *The Institutes*, or the Christ of *The Imitation*, or the Christ of modern biographies;" and well may he say of the wonderful narrative of these gospels, "What stones the building is made of we cannot tell.

One thing is certain. Not only does it contain a true history, but it is a house not made with hands."[1]

Yes, the person is divine and the portraiture is divine. Whenever we see Christ—from the manger to the mount of the ascension—the *Adeste fideles* is our call to all that love him; and our very hearts cry out, "O come, let us adore him!"

"Wherefore God also hath highly exalted him, . . . that at the name of Jesus every knee should bow, of things in heaven, and things in earth, and things under the earth; and that every tongue should confess that Jesus Christ is Lord, to the glory of God the Father."

But the *work* which Christ has done and is doing in the world, through his gospel recorded in the New Testament, is a proof that the record is true and divine—"the record, that God hath given . . . in his son." Not only are the secondary effects wonderful, so that Christendom and civilization are practically coterminous, but there is a greater proof: In millions of human beings— millions multiplying as the ages pass—a work is progressing through which each one is des-

[1] The Church's One Foundation, by W. Robertson Nicoll.

tined to shine forth as the sun in the kingdom he has founded and is bringing to its perfection. The process, in its different stages, is seen in every community, every household, every individual, that has truly received his gospel; and is to the world, looking on, a proof of its truth and divine efficacy. The world beholds sinful men becoming holy, and, lighted with wisdom from on high, walking as children of light.

But the fullest and most joyful proof is reserved for the illumined and the saved, themselves. These, and these only, can say that "God, who commanded the light to shine out of darkness, hath shined in our hearts, to give the light of the knowledge of the glory of God in the face of Jesus Christ." Each of these, and these only, can use Paul's words: "I know him whom I have believed, and I am persuaded that he is able to guard that which I have committed unto him against that day."

MAY WE ALL KNOW THEE, THE ONLY TRUE GOD, AND JESUS CHRIST WHOM THOU HAST SENT.

APPENDIX

NOTE 1
JUSTIN MARTYR'S USE OF THE GOSPELS
1 APOLOGY, CH XV

"*What Christ Himself taught*"—

"Concerning chastity he uttered such sentiments as these. 'Whosoever looketh on a woman to lust after her hath committed adultery with her already in his heart before God'"

"And, 'If thy right eye offend thee, cut it out, for it is better for thee to enter into the kingdom of heaven with one eye than having two eyes to be cast into everlasting fire.'"

"And, 'Whosoever shall marry her that is divorced from another husband committeth adultery.'"

"And, 'There are some who have made themselves eunuchs for the kingdom of heaven's sake, but all cannot receive this saying.' So that, all, who by human law, are twice married, are in the eye of our Master sinners, and those who look upon a woman to lust after her. For not only he who in acts commits adultery is rejected by him, but also he who desires to commit adultery, since not only our works, but also our thoughts, are open before God. And many, both men and women, who have been Christ's disciples from childhood, remain pure at the age of sixty or seventy years, and I boast that I could produce such from every race of men. For, what shall I say, too, of the countless multitude of those who have reformed intemperate habits and learned these things? For Christ called not the just nor the chaste to repentance, but the ungodly and the licentious and the unjust, his words being, 'I came not to call the righteous, but sinners, to repentance.' For the heavenly Father desires rather the repentance than the punishment of the sinner."

"And of our love to all he taught thus 'If ye love them that love you what new thing do ye? For even fornicators do this But I say unto you, pray for your enemies, and love them that hate you, and pray for them that despitefully use you.'"

"And that we should communicate to the needy and do nothing for glory, he said· 'Give to him that asketh, and from him that would borrow turn not away; for if ye lend to them of whom ye hope to receive what new thing do ye? Even the publicans do this Lay not up for yourselves treasure upon earth, where moth and rust doth corrupt, and where robbers break through, but lay up for yourselves treasure in heaven, where neither moth nor rust doth corrupt For, what is a man profited if he shall gain the whole world and lose his own soul? or what shall a man give in exchange for it? Lay up treasure, therefore, where neither moth nor rust doth corrupt '"

"And, 'Be ye kind and merciful, as your Father also is kind and merciful, and maketh his sun to rise on sinners and the righteous and the wicked Take no thought what ye shall eat or what ye shall put on. Are ye not better than the birds and the beasts? And God feedeth them Take no thought, therefore, what ye shall eat or what ye shall put on; for your heavenly Father knoweth that ye have need of these things But seek ye the kingdom of heaven, and all these things shall be added unto you. For where his treasure is, there also is the mind of man '"

"And, 'Do not these things to be seen of men, otherwise, ye have no reward of your father which is in heaven.'"

Appendix 181

One who can read this one chapter of the first *Apology*, and say that Justin did not make use of our gospels must either be demented or possessed of a hardihood truly sublime.

NOTE 2

EARLY USE OF THE GOSPEL OF JOHN

Basilides, the Gnostic (A D. 125), is found quoting the Gospel of John · "That which is said in the gospels ($το λεγόμενον ἐν τοῖς εὐαγγελιοις$) He was the true light which lighteth every man that cometh into the world." Hippolytus' *Refutation of all Heresies*, vii, 10.

$Λεγόμενον$ had just been used by Basilides in quoting Genesis 1: 3, and is used evidently as the equivalent of $γεγραπται$. See *Ante-Nicene Fathers*, Vol. V, p 7. Note

As to the use of the Gospel of John by Polycarp, Papias, Polycrates and other very early writers, which many attempt to explain away by a multitude of suppositions and assumptions, Bishop Lightfoot has this to say ·—

"By a sufficient number of assumptions which lie beyond the range of verification, the evidence may be set aside. But the early existence and recognition of the Fourth Gospel is the one simple postulate that explains all the facts The law of gravitation accounts for the various phenomena of motion—the falling of a stone, the jet of a fountain, the orbits of the planets, etc It is quite possible for anyone, who is disposed, to reject this explanation of nature. Provided that he is allowed to postulate a new force for every new fact with which he is confronted, he has nothing to fear. He will then

> 'gird the sphere
> With centric and concentric scribbled o'er,
> Cycle and epicycle, orb in orb,'

happy in his immunity. But the other theory will prevail, nevertheless, by reason of its simplicity "

NOTE 3

THE LEWIS PALIMPSEST AND THE NEW TESTAMENT TEXT

It is beside the purpose of this little book to enter into any extended discussion of the textual characteristics of the Lewis palimpsest or of any of the documents mentioned. Yet I cannot refrain from suggesting that, while our reliance for the true text must be mainly upon the great uncials, yet in cases where they present insuperable difficulties, and where we find those difficulties removed by this palimpsest which may be the very earliest of all versions, and therefore made from Greek manuscripts much earlier than any to which we have access, its testimony is not to be despised—nay is rather to be welcomed and trusted Two cases which appear to me to be of this kind are Matt. 27. 9 and John 18 28.

The Lewis palimpsest omits "Jeremiah" in the first, and in the second reads thus "But they went not into the judgment-hall, that they should not be defiled whilst they were eating the unleavened bread." The acceptance of these texts relieves two difficulties—the attributing (in our received text) of a quotation from Zechariah to Jeremiah (in Matthew 27 : 9), and confusion as to the time of eating the passover by Christ and his apostles (in John 18 : 28)

The *Diatessaron* also, omits "Jeremiah," but has "passover" in John 18 28. The Lewis palimpsest furnishes the explanation, making the word "passover" here mean the *feast* of the passover—unleavened bread.

NOTE 4

THE DATE OF THE APOLOGY OF ARISTIDES

Professor Harris is inclined to think that the *Apology* was not presented to Hadrian on the occasion named, but either to Hadrian and Antoninus Pius during the few months in A D. 138 when they were colleagues, or to Antoninus

Appendix

alone, after the death of Hadrian. The sign of the plural with the word "majesty" and with the Syriac adjectives for "venerable and merciful," as well as the imperatives "take and read" would incline him to believe that it was addressed to the two emperors, but for the fact that the address "O king" occurs constantly in the *Apology* in the Syriac as well as in the Greek and the Armenian. This inclines him to believe that these plurals are erroneous and that the *Apology* was probably addressed to Antoninus Pius alone after the death of Hadrian.

In such a case we can only weigh, as best we may, the probabilities.

We know, for one thing, that it is not unusual to find interpolations and other changes in writings of the second century, especially in translations. This Syriac copy of the *Apology* abounds in them, and if we make the not improbable supposition that this second address and the plurals named are of this character, then there is absolutely nothing to keep us from believing that the *Apology* was addressed to Hadrian in the eighth year of his reign.

The first address of this Syriac copy, it must be remembered, is "Here follows the defense which Aristides the philosopher made *before Hadrian the king* on behalf of reverence for God," while that of the Armenian fragment reads "*To the Emperor Cæsar Hadrian* from Aristides." The address is not in the Greek because of its incorporation in the story of Barlaam and Josaphat, but it begins, "I, O King," etc., the original Greek thus showing that it was addressed to only one sovereign.

To accept the conclusion of Professor Harris, in the words of the *Introduction* to the *Apology of Aristides* in the *Ante-Nicene Fathers*, "requires us to suppose that Eusebius was wrong, that Jerome copied his error; [and it must be remembered that Jerome says that it was extant in his day, and his description of it would seem to indicate his personal knowledge of it] that the Armenian version curiously fell into the same mistake, and that the Syriac translation is, at this point, exceptionally faithful."

Now, it is extremely improbable that Eusebius who states that it was presented to Hadrian, should have been mistaken in this case. The *Apology* was well known in his day, and copies of it seem to have been abundant—"preserved by *a great number* even to the present day," are his words. But, what would seem fairly decisive, he tells us that he had in his hands the *Apology* of Aristides' companion apologist, Quadratus He *must* have seen with his own eyes to whom *this* was addressed, and he says it was Hadrian.

Besides, "a hearer of the apostles" as Quadratus is said to have been, could hardly have lived long after A. D. 124-6

In addition to this, the *character* of the *Apology* indicates its early origin.

Dr Harris himself gives the following view of the indications as to the date of the *Apology* in its style and contents ·

"The simplicity of the style of the *Apology* is in favor of an early date The religious ideas and practices are of an antique cast The ethics show a remarkable continuity with Jewish ethics the care for the stranger and the friendless, the burial of the dead, and the like, are given as characteristic virtues both of Judaism and Christianity. Indeed we may say that one of the surprising things about the *Apology* is the friendly tone in which the Jews are spoken of One certainly would not suspect that the chasm between the Church and the Synagogue had become as practically impassable as we find it in the middle of the second century. There is no sign of the hostility to the Jews which we find in the *Martyrdom of Polycarp*, and nothing like the severity of contempt which we find in the *Epistle to Diognetus* If the Church is not, in the writer's time, under the wing of the Synagogue, it apparently has no objection to taking the Synagogue occasionally under its own wing

"Such a consideration seems to be a mark of antiquity, and one would, therefore, prefer to believe, if it were possible, that the *Apology* was earlier than the revolt under Bar-Cocheba." (*Texts and Studies*, vol. 1, No. 1, p 13)

The editor of Cambridge *Texts and Studies*, Dr. J Armitage Robinson, thinks it entirely " possible " to believe it, in spite of the second title, in view of the fact that the translator of the Greek *Apology* into Syriac has dealt very freely with his original, expunging some things, and adding so many others that the Syriac occupies half as much space again as the Greek. He says in his appendix (*Texts and Studies*, vol. 1, No. 1, p. 75, note). " Mr. Harris inclines to accept this second title as the true one, but the course of the present argument tends to show that the Syriac translator has introduced many arbitrary changes on his own account and this makes me more unwilling to accept his testimony as against that of the Armenian version, which has, moreover, the explicit statement of Eusebius to support it."

He also notes the fact that the Armenian fragment shows a much closer correspondence with the original Greek than does the Syriac where the two merely translate. "The explicit statement of Eusebius " in his *Chronicon* is thus given by Dr. Harris —

" 1. The Armenian version of the *Chronicon* gives under the year A D 124, as follows —

        Ol   A abr   Imp Rom.
        d226   2140   8e

dAdrianus Eleusinarum verum gnarus fuit multaque (dona) Atheniensium largitus est

eRomanorum ecclesiæ episcopatum excipit septimus Telesphorus annis XI

" Codratus, apostolorum auditor, et Aristides, nostri dogmatis (nostræ vel) philosophus atheniensis, dedere apologeticas (apologiæ, responsionis) ob mandatum." The occasion and the substance of the mandate concerning the Christians, the "Rescript of Hadrian," is then given

Dr. Armitage Robinson gives very clearly the evidence that "the Armenian version is not made from the Syriac version in its present form," and remarks that "similar arguments could be adduced if there were any necessity, to show that the Syriac version is independent of the Armenian"

The Armenian version, then, is an *independent authority* for the address to Hadrian alone.

Dr Robinson shows the unreliableness of the Syriac version by comparing it with a Syriac version of the *Oratio ad Græcos* ascribed to Justin, in which he says, "Variation begins to show itself immediately after the first sentence" In this *Oratio* he shows, too, how the Syriac translator inserted particulars not in the original, evidently to vaunt his independent knowledge A similar attempt seems to have been made by the Syriac translator of the *Apology*, or a copyist, in inserting the duplicate address, possibly because of a tradition that it was presented to Antoninus Pius after its presentation to Hadrian [1]

Dr Harris notes a serious error in punctuation in the first sentence of the Syriac and is inclined to think that the sign of the plural is a mistake, expressing the opinion that the *Apology* was addressed to Antoninus Pius alone, after Hadrian's reign. In order to make this consistent with the fact that Quadratus delivered an *Apology* at the same time, he has either to identify Quadratus with a bishop of Athens of that name who flourished about 170, or, else, to suppose that the two *Apologies* were delivered at different times to different emperors

I think all will agree that the evidence, both from the

[1] "If . = 'Renewed, or dedicated again to . . Antoninus Pius,' could be read, both headings might be retained."—*Ante-Nicene Fathers*, vol. ix, p 263, note

Appendix 187

clear statements of Eusebius and from the documents themselves, is reasonably conclusive that Aristides, an Athenian philosopher, and Quadratus, an "*auditor apostolorum,*" delivered their *Apologies* to Hadrian at Athens in the eighth year of his reign, A D 124-126 The other view requires too many improbable suppositions and readjustments to make it at all credible.

NOTE 5
THE NEW TESTAMENT AND THE CLASSICS

The great advantages we enjoy for determining the text of the New Testament may be seen when we remember the vast number of quotations from it by writers of the second and third centuries, the large number of versions of it in several languages and the many early manuscripts of it which still exist The case of the Latin and Greek classics presents a marked contrast, as the following extract from the curator of manuscripts in the British Museum, Frederic George Kenyon, D Lit , Ph D., will show " But of the classics we have no original autographs, nor any copies nearly contemporaneous with them The intervals which separate the composition of the great classics from the date of the earliest extant manuscripts of them must be numbered by hundreds, and sometimes by thousands of years. The plays of Æschylus were written between 485 and 450 B C and the earliest extant manuscript of them (a few unimportant scraps excepted) was written in the eleventh century— an interval of some 1,500 years. For Sophocles, for Thucydides, for Herodotus, the interval is substantially the same, for Pindar and Euripides it extends to 1,600 years For Plato, we have interesting fragments of two of his dialogues written only a century after his death , but for the greater part of his works we are dependent on manuscripts eleven hundred years later. Aristotle (except for his recently recovered history of the Athenian Constitution) is in a similar case; the earliest manuscript of the *Ethics* was written in the tenth century, while for the Politics we have no complete copy earlier than the fourteenth. We are better off in regard to some of the Latin writers. Virgil, who died 19 B. C., is represented by several manuscripts which may be assigned to the fifth century, or even to the fourth; considerable portions of Livy exist in copies of the fifth and sixth centuries; there is a precious (though badly damaged) manuscript of Plautus which belongs to the fourth century; while there are fragments of Cicero which may go back to an even earlier date. But, for Tacitus, we have an interval of 750 years before we reach our earliest copy of him, for Horace and Lucretius, 900 years; while in the case of Catullus the most spontaneously poetic spirit in all the literature of Rome, we are dependent upon a few manuscripts written nearly 1,450 years after his death. It is worth while to note, in passing, how greatly superior in respect of antiquity of attestation is the Greek Testament. The shortest interval which separates any classical author from any substantial manuscript of his works is some 400 years, while in the majority of cases, it ranges from 1,000 to 1,500 years, but of the New Testament we have complete copies within 250 years of the date at which many of the books composing it were written."

Again he says, "Virgil is the only classical author whose text is on the same footing as that of the New Testament, it being mainly based on uncial manuscripts. There are three substantially complete manuscripts of Virgil written in capitals (which differ from uncials only in being of squarer and stiffer formation). Besides these, there are three imperfect manuscripts in the same style, and though this amount of uncial evidence is incomparably less than in the case of the New Testament, it is much greater than is found in any other classical writer."—From article in *Harper's Magazine*, August, 1902, on *The Lineage of the Classics*.

The advantage of the New Testament in the matter of

Appendix

manuscripts could hardly be better stated in a few words than we find it given in the following extract —

"A few precious copies written on vellum or parchment have come down to us from a very early period, the most important of which are (1) the Vatican, styled Codex B, preserved in the Vatican Library at Rome, and dating from the fourth century, (2) the Sinaitic Codex discovered by Tischendorf in St. Catherine Convent at the foot of Mt. Sinai in 1859, now deposited at St. Petersburg, likewise of the fourth century, (3) the Alexandrine (Codex A), preserved in the British Museum, and dating from the fifth century. These, and other ancient manuscripts to the number of about a hundred are called Uncials, because written with capital letters without any separation between the words—the others of a more modern character being called Cursives, because written in a running hand Of the latter there are about two thousand, an immense array of witnesses compared with the few manuscripts of classical works preserved to us, which can generally be counted on the ten fingers "—McGlymont's *New Testament and its writers*, small ed , pp 2, 3

The author does not mention Codex D (Codex Bezæ), now brought into special prominence by Nestle, Harris and others.

In a later article in the same magazine (Nov 1902), Mr. Kenyon says —

"We owe our knowledge of most of the great works of Greek and Latin literature—Æschylus, Sophocles, Thucydides, Horace, Lucretius, Tacitus, and many more—to manuscripts written from 900 to 1,500 years after their authors' deaths ; while of the New Testament we have two excellent and approximately complete copies at an interval of only 250 years. Again, of the classical writers we have as a rule, only a few score of copies (often less), of which one or two stand out as decisively superior to the rest ; but of the

New Testament we have more than 3,000 copies (besides the very large number of versions), and many of these have distinct and independent value."

But the versions, in various languages, form a valuable source of information as to the original text of the New Testament. "In spite of the ravages of time, more than three thousand copies of the Greek New Testament, whole or in part, still exist; and to these must be added the copies of the early translations into other languages—Syriac, Coptic, Armenian, Gothic, Latin, etc.—which give invaluable assistance to the scholar in ascertaining the correct text of the Scriptures."

Besides all this, early Christian writings which have come down to us with the words of the New Testament imbedded and preserved in them not only prove the existence of it in their day, but indicate its text. It has been asserted by a competent scholar that he has found by personal examination two-thirds of the New Testament in the extant remnant of the Greek writings of Origen alone, as one instance. This source of evidence is almost entirely lacking in the case of the classics.

NOTE 6

THE SO-CALLED GOSPEL ACCORDING TO THE HEBREWS

Some readers may wish to know more about the so-called *Gospel according to the Hebrews*, as a certain class of scholars are disposed to urge its claims to something like equality with the canonical gospels, while some infidels, as we have seen, assert its priority in date to all of them.

An article in the *Biblical World* for September, 1902, claims that it was identical with the Hebrew *Logia* of Matthew mentioned by Papias (about A D 140), who says, as quoted by Eusebius (H. E III, xxxix), "Matthew composed his history in the Hebrew dialect, and every one

Appendix

translated it as he was able." The writer represents this as the view of most modern scholars.

As we have seen above, Dr Bernhard Weiss unhesitatingly affirms that it has no connection with this work (which Hilgenfeld and many other scholars think never really existed except in the misguided imagination of the weak-minded Papias) and shows that the fragments of the *Gospel according to the Hebrews* are taken from the three synoptic gospels, while there are evident traces of the gospel of John in words or expressions peculiar to that gospel —all being changed, of course, to sustain the views of the Ebionites or the Nazarenes who used them. The same passages vary much in different recensions of this so-called gospel, as is shown especially in the different accounts given in different copies quoted by Epiphanius and Jerome It should be remembered that our synoptic gospels were over three hundred years old when the *Gospel of the Hebrews* was quoted by Epiphanius, and still older when quoted by Jerome, so that the heretics of these centuries had had ample time to manipulate and change them according to their various or changing ideas. The differences in the accounts of the baptism of Christ and the descent of the Holy Spirit upon him show this with special clearness. By this time, too, these errorists had set up the claim that the *Gospel according to the Hebrews* was the work of the apostle Matthew.

Now, the discovery of the *Diatessaron of Tatian* and the Lewis palimpsest of the four gospels has made the whole matter plain, and strange to say, the writer of the article in the *Biblical World* does not mention these discoveries at all If, throughout the *Diatessaron*, composed soon after A. D. 150, our four gospels alone are used—and this is the case—then there is the proof that they and they alone were the gospels of the Christian world at that period, just as Irenæus testifies that they were in his time, fifty years later.

The Lewis palimpsest, too, has our four gospels alone. If the *Diatessaron* and the *palimpsest* had contained the peculiar readings of the *Gospel according to the Hebrews*, a certain class of critics would have been jubilant. Now, they are entirely silent about these discoveries and act as if they had nothing to do with the matter, when, in fact, they present the clearest proof that our gospels alone were the gospels of the Christian world during the half century after the death of the last of the apostles. Nicholson, who wrote his elaborate treatise on the *Gospel according to the Hebrews* before these discoveries were made, used great diligence in gathering and arranging the thirty fragments which he thought certainly belonged to this so-called gospel, together with thirty-four others which he thought probably or possibly belonged to it. But when he comes to marshaling these fragments and interpreting their peculiarities in the endeavor to sustain his theory that Matthew wrote, at one time, the Hebrew Gospel (which Nicholson identifies with this *Gospel according to the Hebrews*), and at another time, our canonical Greek Matthew, he reminds one much more of an adept in the arts of legerdemain than of a sober reasoner. The legitimate conclusion from the facts which he adduces is that which is made clear by the discovery of the *Diatessaron* and the palimpsest—namely, that the *Gospel according to the Hebrews* is a heretical document drawn from our gospels, with additions, omissions and changes of text, and not recognized by the Christian Church at the middle of the second century.

NOTE 7

Harnack's Honest Acknowledgment

In a review of Dr Armitage Robinson's book, *The Study of the Gospels*, *The Churchman*, London, has this to say (Sep., 1902) —

Appendix

"He [Dr Robinson], mentions moreover, that Dr. Harnack, in sending to him his own *Chronology of Early Christian Literature*, in which he 'approximates to the older views,' wrote that ' he hoped that, as to its main positions, we should find ourselves in agreement, and that differences would henceforward appear in the interpretation of the books rather than in the problems of their date and authenticity.'

"It is, in fact, an immense gain to the Christian argument that the most distinguished ecclesiastical scholar in Germany has substantially admitted the truth of the tradition of the Church respecting the dates, and to a great extent, the authorship of the books of the New Testament. The German criticism, which, toward the end of the last century, used to be thrown at the heads of ' Apologists ' in England by such controversialists as the late Professor Huxley, is now acknowledged in Germany itself—in Berlin itself —to have been mistaken , and the result of the controversy for fifty years is the rehabilitation, in the most important points, of the ancient Christian tradition."

www.ingramcontent.com/pod-product-compliance
Lightning Source LLC
Chambersburg PA
CBHW051051160426
43193CB00010B/1141